From CLEARANCE TO PRICELESS

A Main Karacter™ Guide to Getting off
the Clearance Rack and Reclaiming Your Worth

KARA VAVAL

Disclaimer:
This book is for informational and educational purposes only and is not intended as medical advice, diagnosis, or treatment. Always seek the advice of a qualified healthcare professional regarding any medical condition or health-related decisions.
The author and publisher disclaim any liability for any adverse effects resulting from the use or application of the information contained in this book.

DEDICATION

I dedicate this book to the girl I once was. The one who walked through confusion, heartbreak and uncertainty, without a map, without a manual or a safety net—this is for you. You carried more than anyone saw and still found a way to keep going. You protected me the only ways you knew how. You made brave choices with limited information, trusted your instincts when no one else was guiding you, and learned lessons the hard way so I could stand here wiser and stronger. Your resilience became my foundation. Your courage became my compass. I honor the fight in you, the faith you scraped together on the hard days, and the wisdom you gathered along the way. Thank you for getting us here. You don't have to carry it all anymore, I've got it from here and I will never forget that everything I am is built on everything you survived. I love you.

And to my two incredible children, Luc & Lia. You have journeyed with me through my highs and my lows, witnessing the many versions of me along the way. Your patience, your grace, and your unconditional love have been my unwavering anchor. You are my greatest teachers and my greatest joy. Thank you. I love you.

TABLE OF
CONTENTS

FOREWORD

by Lisa Nichols

I met Kara by what many would call coincidence, but what I know in my soul was divine appointment. Unbeknownst to me, my team had connected with her just a few short weeks earlier about attending one of my upcoming events, and although the dots didn't quite connect at first, destiny had other plans. I was in the lobby of the Shore Club in Turks and Caicos, about to check in, when Kara, who was about to check out, quite literally crossed paths with me. In that serendipitous moment, it became abundantly clear that a force greater than both of us was at play, orchestrating our coming together.

Two weeks later, Kara was in my living room for our first executive coaching mastermind. She has since participated in several programs on my campus, and I've witnessed her courage, her healing, her tenacity, and her unrelenting decision to become who she was always meant to be. I watched her do the deep inner work, peel back the layers of old narratives, and reclaim her power and brilliance. The book you now hold in your hands is the fruit of that journey.

Every woman's journey to self-worth looks different, but the lessons along the way often sound the same: courage, forgiveness, healing, and truth. In From Clearance to Priceless, Kara offers her perspective on these universal themes with honesty and heart. She invites readers to take a brave look at their own lives and rediscover the value that was never truly lost, only forgotten.

What stands out in this book is its blend of vulnerability and practicality. Kara doesn't simply tell her story; she uses it as a bridge to yours. Each chapter offers both reflection and invitation, giving you the chance to see yourself in her experiences and to gather tools that move you toward greater wholeness.

As someone who has spent decades guiding others through transformation, I recognize the power of the principles she shares. Self-worth, personal responsibility, forgiveness, and faith are not theories. They are daily practices that free us to live in alignment with our true value. Kara's journey illustrates what happens when we choose to believe that everything, even our hardest moments, can work for our good.

This book is a timely reminder that your story, with all its detours and delays, is still sacred. Whether you are healing from heartbreak, rediscovering your confidence, or learning to dream again, From Clearance to Priceless will remind you that you've never been discounted, only in the process of becoming.

So read these pages slowly. Let the insights take root. And remember, you were never meant to live on the clearance rack. You are, and have always been, priceless.

Lisa Nichols
CEO, Motivating the Masses
Author of No Matter What! and Abundance Now

INTRODUCTION

I am writing this book because it is the book I wish someone had placed in my hands in my late teens or early twenties as an honest guide of "what to expect from" and "how to" navigate this game we call life.

As I sit here to write these opening pages, I look back on my life, and a wave of emotions flood my body. I am deeply proud of the woman I have become.

Today, I am an accomplished attorney, a devoted mother, businesswoman and coach to high-performing women. I am a supportive and loving sister, cousin and niece; I'm also the cool auntie, a reliable friend to my small circle and a champion and advocate for women who are reclaiming their worth, restoring their confidence, and creating lives that inspire them. When I look at myself, I see a solid human.

I am the woman of my dreams.

Tears stream down my face as I write this because becoming her was not easy. The road that led me here was anything but smooth. It demanded courage I did not always believe I had, strength that was often built in moments of despair, and faith that sometimes felt shaky. Growth asked more of me than comfort ever could.

I am a month shy of my 43rd birthday as I write these lines and for nearly thirty years, I have been making my way to this very moment.

I was only 14 years old when my father was brutally murdered back home in Haiti. Four short years later, my grandmother died in a house fire. Loss found me early, and it did not come gently.

In the spirit of surviving these early life blows, I did what I thought I was supposed to do. I checked all the boxes. I double-majored in college, went to law school and got married at twenty-two to a "nice guy" that I would subsequently divorce at thirty-six. I kept moving, kept achieving, kept proving to myself and to the world that I was strong, refusing to be defeated by life which had already tried to break me.

The six-and-a-half-year relationship I was in after my marriage recently ended in betrayal and heartbreak. This is the man I believed to be my soul-mate, the love of my life, the one I thought I would spend the rest of my life with. That breakup hurt me in a deep and consuming way. It cracked me open and forced me to finally sit with myself to feel everything I had once pushed aside just to keep going. The pain was awful but necessary. This book is the fruit of my healing.

I have had to pull myself up by my bootstraps more times than I can count. Still, by the grace of God, my heart remained pure, and my spirit never stopped searching for light. Even in my darkest moments, something in me refused to give up. I kept believing there was meaning in the pain, that nothing was wasted.

Somehow, I always knew everything was happening for a reason, a reason that would one day make sense. A reason I could not see then, but one that has become clear now.

Why am I telling you this?

Well, that is because you and I are not so different.

The details of our lives may be different. The faces, places, and moments that shaped your story may be different from mine. But like me, you have known pain. You have faced trials, betrayals, confusion, and lessons you never asked for. Like me, you have had to keep going even when the weight felt heavy. Like me, you have been becoming.

And wherever this book meets you, whether you are standing at the beginning of your healing, sitting in the middle of your questions, or quietly rebuilding after loss, I want you to hear this clearly: you are perfect, whole and complete, just the way you are and just the way you are not. You are not broken and there is nothing wrong with you. If fact, everything is right with you and you lack nothing.

You are exactly who you were meant to be, both in who you are now and in who you are still becoming. There is nothing you could have done to rewrite your past. Nothing you missed. Nothing you failed to fix. Every moment, every joy, every mistake, and every wound, played a role in shaping the person you are today. None of it was wasted.

If you are asking, "Why me?" If things feel unclear, unfair, or painfully confusing right now, I want you to stay with me.

Keep reading.

What feels senseless today will find meaning in time. What hurts now will soon make you wiser.

In the meantime, while the puzzle pieces are still coming together, may I offer you the perspective that has carried me through the years? It is the one belief that has kept me in the driver's seat of my life, even when nothing made sense, when I felt lost, broken, confused, and bone tired.

No matter what is happening in my life, I remain anchored in one truth: everything is happening for me, not to me.

I believe there is a Life Force behind all of this, whether you call it God or the Universe. It is that omnipotent, limitless, expansive force that keeps the sun rising each morning and setting each night. The same force that keeps trees rooted, creatures breathing, and life unfolding. That force created you. It created me, too; my background, my heart, my mind, my strengths and weaknesses, my skills, my talents, and even my flaws. Likewise, for you.

If that is true, then my life could not be accidental and your life could not be accidental. There had to be an intention behind it. A Purpose. A Meaning.

And if that is the case, then there could be no other explanation for everything we have lived through other than: it was exactly what was needed. Every experience was training, character development preparing me for my life's purpose, for the calling I am uniquely equipped to fulfill. And so, it is for you.

The people.
The circumstances.
The highs and the lows.
The plot twists.
The heartbreaks and the wins.
The losses and the lessons.

Every single moment happened because it was necessary for my becoming.

Truthfully, I love the woman I have become on the other side of this journey, no matter how painful or demanding it has been. I cannot celebrate who I am now while rejecting the road that lead me here. Nor can I become all I am meant to be if I keep resisting the challenges still ahead. All I can do is trust the process. I can keep showing up for my life, allowing each experience to shape and guide me, with the clear understanding that no one is coming to save me, and that, in truth, I no longer want to be saved.

From Clearance to Priceless is both a figurative and a literal title. For years, I lived with a deep sense of low self-worth, shaped by early losses and what felt like abandonment. That pain, and the constant fear of being left again, led me to tolerate people, behaviors, and situations that diminished me. I lived on life's clearance rack, undervaluing myself, settling for less, and believing love and success were things I had to earn or accept with conditions attached.

It was only when I chose to do the hard, honest work of reclaiming my value that something shifted. I finally understood that I was never meant to be discounted. I was never meant to shrink myself to fit what others could offer. I was, and always have been, priceless. And now, you are being invited to do that same work for yourself.

And then there was the very real scarcity I lived in for years, the kind I created and carried with me. The stress of stretching a single dollar. The quiet fear of not having enough. The constant mental math of what could be paid for and what had to wait. Scarcity didn't just sit in my bank account; it took up space in my mind. It shaped what I believed I deserved and what I thought was possible for me.

It wasn't until my early to mid-thirties that something began to shift. I slowly moved from a mindset of lack to one of abundance, not only financially, but in every area of my life. That change lifted me off the clearance rack of survival and placed me into the priceless realm of overflow. This is where I live now, and it is where I guide other women to step into as well.

This book is both my story and your invitation.

As you go through these pages, I invite you to let the words, stories, and lessons sink in. Allow them to settle into your mind and gently reshape the way you think.

Take a moment to take a good look at yourself in the mirror, because this is the last time you will meet this version of you. By the time you close this book, you will have grown beyond the person staring back at you now. Today is the first day of the rest of your life. Let's begin.

CHAPTER 1

YOU ARE THE MAIN KARACTER™
YOU WERE BORN WORTHY

"All the world's a stage, and all the men and women merely players; They have their exits and their entrances; And one man in his time plays many parts."

—William Shakespeare

You've probably heard it said before: you are the main character in the story of your life. But have you truly paused to ponder the depth and weight of that statement? Have you considered that the people who appear and disappear from your life are merely supporting actors, playing their parts to help move your story forward?

Think of them as guest stars, stepping in and out, each casted into a role meant to challenge you, teach you, or illuminate a part of yourself you hadn't yet discovered. Every encounter, every relationship, no matter how brief or long-lasting, exists to shape your journey and help you grow into the person you were always meant to be.

Shakespeare captured this beautifully: "All the world's a stage, and all the men and women merely players. They have their exits and entrances; and one man in his time plays many parts, his acts being seven ages."

Think about the last movie you watched. Who was the main character? Can you see how the actions of every other character, in one way or another, pointed back to the main character?

When you watch a movie, especially one built around a hero's journey, you spend about ninety minutes witnessing a rich mix of people, places, and moments, all carefully woven around a single life. Characters enter and exit. Circumstances rise and fall. Yet everything that happens serves one purpose: to move the story forward and shape the main character into who they are becoming.

As the story unfolds, the main character is tested, stretched, broken, and rebuilt. Each encounter leaves a mark. Each challenge adds depth. Nothing appears by accident. Every person and every situation plays a role in the unfolding of that journey.

Now pause for a moment and turn that lens inward.

Have you ever considered that the same quiet process has been happening in your own life all these years?

What if you are the main character of your story, not by chance, but by design? What if the people you've met, the places you've passed through, and the circumstances that have shaped you were not random interruptions, but essential parts of your becoming?

Is it really so far-fetched to imagine that every experience, both the ones that lifted you and the ones that nearly broke you, arrived when it did because it was needed? Needed to shape you. Needed to grow you. Needed to prepare you for the unique story that only you can live.

Truth is, you were born whole, already carrying everything you need to play the main role in the story of your life. Nothing that has happened to you was a mistake. Life has not been happening to you; it has been happening for you all along. There was nothing you could have done to change, edit, or rewrite the script unfolding behind your story.

What you see as flaws or shortcomings are not errors in design. They are the very traits that make you the only one qualified to play this role. They shape your depth, your voice, your strength. They make you the perfect actor for your own life. Even the heroes and villains in your story played their parts exactly as they needed to. Each encounter, each wound, each lesson helped shape and develop you into who you are becoming.

Maybe you were never broken.
Maybe this was always part of your origin story.

And with that understanding comes a quiet freedom. The greatest gift you can give yourself is permission to relax into your life, to stop fighting the plot and start trusting the unfolding. To live not as someone desperately trying to control the story, but as an aware participant, fully present and awake within it.

Show up, participate and engage as life invites you to.

Hold on to nothing. Resist nothing. Control nothing.

As you do, you will find yourself standing at the doorway of true peace, not because everything turned out the way you wanted, but because you finally stopped needing it to. And in that letting go, happiness no longer feels distant or fragile. It feels lived.

The main character in the movie of my life? Her name is Kara. Her story begins in Flushing, Queens, New York, on September 9, 1982.

I am the middle child of three. My parents, both originally from Haiti, met and married in New York, where they began their life together. When I was just six months old, they decided to relocate back to Haiti. That is where I grew up and, by many accounts, lived a fairly charmed childhood.

My dad was larger than life. From a very young age, I remember being completely mesmerized by his presence. He was a man's man and a lady's man, an incomparable provider with vision not only for his family, but for his country. He was a hard worker, a hustler in the truest sense, a dependable friend, and a joyful spirit with a raw yet refreshing sense of humor.

He was unforgettable, the kind of human being who felt different the moment you stepped into his space.

Everything changed on November 9, 1996. I was fourteen years old. My father was forty-two.

While at work for a coffee company, he was brutally murdered. In that single moment, the life I knew ended. My father left behind my then forty-year-old mother, my seventeen-year-old sister, my five-year-old brother, and me. In the blink of an eye, my mother became a single parent of three children, with the main provider of our home suddenly gone.

To this day, I can still see the disorientation in her eyes. She did the best she could, but even then, I instinctively knew I needed to step up, to help raise my little brother, to help carry the weight of what had fallen apart. I became an adult overnight. I didn't have the luxury, time or space to *feel* anything. New responsibilities arrived all at once, and survival took over.

I didn't know it then, but something else was born the day my father was murdered. A new identity formed inside me, one rooted in survival. You may recognize it. I call it the *strong woman* identity.

That identity shielded me. It protected me from drowning in grief and from the pain of losing my father. It also guarded me from an abandonment wound I wouldn't recognize until much later. I had to be strong, not just for myself, but for my mother and my siblings. There was no room to fall apart, no capacity to process grief—so I kept going.

On one hand, that identity allowed me to function. On the other hand, it carried a wound that followed me for nearly thirty years. I didn't realize it then, but it quietly ran many areas of my life, especially my relationships. More on that later.

Recently, I heard someone say, *If you don't address your childhood wounds, your relationships will.* I can attest to the truth of that statement.

Two years passed, and I knew I could not stay in Haiti any longer. In August 1999, just one month before my seventeenth birthday, and against my mother's wishes, I moved to Queens, New York, to live with my maternal grandmother. I needed to finish high school and find a path forward.

I could no longer live in a place where my father had been murdered, where the perpetrators were known, yet still walked freely in the streets where justice never came.

My grandmother welcomed me with open arms. At seventy-one, however, she had no idea how to navigate the school system. I had to figure it out myself. I figured out how to enroll in a safe high school, since the neighborhood one was not an option, and later, how to get myself into college.

I graduated from Francis Lewis High School in Fresh Meadows, New York, in June 2000. That September, I began college at Adelphi University in Garden City, New York. I received an "opportunity" scholarship based on my story and the hardship I had endured after losing my father. The condition was that I had to live on campus.

Even though my grandmother's home was only ten minutes away, I stayed in the dorms during the week and went home on weekends.

Two months into my freshman year, on November 18, 2000, I decided to stay on campus that Friday night. A friend was visiting from New Jersey, and I changed my plans.

That night, my grandmother's house caught fire.

She did not survive.

Unfathomable... For a time, I truly believed God had a personal vendetta against me. I wondered what I could have possibly done—what sin from some past life I was paying for—that so much loss could keep finding me so early.

Once again, I had to be strong.

There was even less room to grieve now, less capacity to process another loss. This one just layered itself onto my already existing abandonment wounds, adding to the trauma that had already lodged itself deep into my body.

I was eighteen years old and felt as though I had already lived an entire lifetime of chaos and pain.

I clung to the phrase *everything happens for a reason* and kept moving. For the next four years, I buried myself in my studies, taking eighteen credits a semester while working three jobs. Then I went on to law school for another three years.

I don't know your origin story. But I do know this: just like me, you were born into circumstances you did not choose, and those circumstances shaped you. Every plot twist, challenge, pain, healing, triumph and growth was all character development for a divine screenplay written specifically for you.

This life, this body, this journey, it was assigned to you—on purpose. And with that assignment came a role that no one else can play.

You don't need to audition for it.
You don't need to qualify for it.
You don't need to earn it.

You were cast the moment you arrived.

Again, you are perfect, whole, and complete just as you are and just as you are not for this role that belongs only to you. There is no backup actor. No stand-in. No substitute.

You are the lead. The main *Kara*cter™.

Everything you have been through, every loss, every detour, every doubt, is part of the script. Not to break you, but to build you into the version of yourself capable of embodying the role you came here to play. Your voice, your presence, and your power were forged through what you survived.

When you fully understand this, when you decide to own your story without trying to fix, prove, or polish yourself into worthiness, something shifts. When you claim your flaws, your scars, and your fears, you step fully into the main character you have always been.

And once you see it, you can finally live the purpose you were built for.

The main character role of your life has already been cast.

You got the part.

This is your movie.
This is your moment.

CHAPTER 2

LIFE HAPPENS FOR YOU,
NOT TO YOU

"Life is simple. Everything happens for you, not to you. Everything happens at exactly the right moment, neither too soon nor too late. You don't have to like it... It's just easier if you do."

— Byron Katie

My daughter recently asked me a question that stopped me in my tracks. She wanted to know if there was one thing I could change about my life, what would it be?

I paused.

In that quiet moment, memories rushed in. My father's murder. Marrying my first husband. The pain, the loss, the versions of myself I had to outgrow just to survive. All of it flashed through my mind in seconds. And yet, when I finally answered her, my response surprised even me.

Nothing.

I wouldn't change a thing.

I love the woman I am today, and every part of my journey, every joy, every heartbreak, every hard lesson, is the reason she exists. My life unfolded exactly the way it needed to, leading me to this very moment, to this version of myself that feels grounded, aware, and whole in ways I once didn't think were possible.

That doesn't mean I didn't have other plans for myself. I did. But I also get why my life unfolded the way it did.

I never planned to lose my father at such a young age. I never planned to get divorced. I never imagined enduring the kind of devastating, disorienting heartbreak that comes from loving someone deeply, believing they were "the one," only to watch that future fall apart.

But what if those moments weren't meant to break us?

What if the plot twists, the detours, the losses, and the heartbreaks were never punishments at all?

What if they were assignments?

Life has been unfolding exactly the way it was always meant to and every unexpected detour shaped you into the woman you were destined to become. Nothing has been accidental, and you were never "holding it together." Even the chapters you wish you could erase were delivering lessons, mirrors, and momentum.

And yet, somewhere along the journey, you convinced yourself that it should have looked different. That it should have felt easier. That it should not have hurt as much. But who told you that? Who said it was supposed to be different from what it is?

The truth is, life has been doing its job all along. The real question is whether you are willing to see the perfection in the path that brought you here. Life is not happening *to* you. Life is happening *for* you.

A year after graduating from college, I got married and moved to South Florida to attend law school. I was checking all the right boxes, following the script I believed would lead me to happiness. Then life handed me a plot twist.

After graduating from law school, I sat for the Florida Bar. While waiting for the results, I discovered I had passed a different test altogether—a pregnancy test.

That pregnancy changed everything.

I went from dreaming of making partner at the boutique securities litigation firm where I worked to wanting one thing only: to be a mom. When my unpaid maternity leave came to an end three months after my son arrived, I found myself at a crossroads. I needed to earn money, but I could not stomach the thought of missing my son's milestones just to put money in someone else's pocket. The salary was not worth the precious, irreplaceable time I knew I would lose.

A decision had to be made.

So, I did the one thing I have always relied on when my back is against the wall.

I prayed...

My prayers were answered when a woman walked up to me at a local Target and offered me a facial with Mary Kay® cosmetics. By the end of our time together, I had become a Mary Kay consultant. Yes, me. A brand-new, Florida-licensed attorney chose to sell skincare and color cosmetics so she could have the time freedom to be the kind of mother she wanted to be.

My starter kit cost $100. For just $100, I bought my freedom and walked away from the traditional legal career path, betting on myself and on entrepreneurship. And guess what? I made my first six figures through that business. Even more incredible, that beauty business funded the law firm I still run almost seventeen years later, as I write these words.

At the time, it felt like a detour, maybe even a step backward. I believed I was leaving behind the prestige I had worked so hard to earn. But within that so-called detour, I discovered a gift I never could have planned for: the ability to empower women.

As I built my Mary Kay® business, I realized I wasn't just passionate about selling products. I was deeply drawn to inspiring women—to helping them believe in themselves and recognize their own beauty, strength, and potential. Something that began as a temporary hustle soon informed me that it was actually a calling.

That calling eventually led me to build my Laptop Lifestyle Lawyer® brand, through which I help women lawyers break free from traditional law jobs and create virtual law firms that provide them with financial independence, time freedom, and the opportunity to build a life on their own terms, just as I did.

Can you see how the unexpected plot twist of my pregnancy, how what looked like life knocking me off track, was actually life preparing me for my true purpose? Everything unfolded so perfectly, leading me exactly where I was meant to go professionally, not where I thought I was supposed to end up.

As you read this, you may already be thinking of moments in your own life that did not go according to plan: the job that didn't work out, the relationship that ended, the door that closed when you were certain it would open. I want to invite you to pause and look back at those moments through a different lens.

What if those detours were not derailments, but divine redirections? What if every "no," every heartbreak, and every unexpected twist was life's gentle—or sometimes not-so-gentle— way of guiding you toward your purpose? When you begin to trace the thread that connects the moments of your past, you may see something surprising: life has been working for you all along, not against you.

I know, I know. Sometimes this truth is hard to accept, especially when the plot twist comes through heartbreak, grief, or loss. But I am here to tell you this, having lived through each of them myself: it is all happening for you.

As painful, disorienting, and traumatic as it was, losing my father and grandmother early in life forced me to tap into a reservoir of courage I didn't even know existed within me. Had I grown up with their continued presence and support, I may never have developed the hustle and resourcefulness that can only be forged through survival. Their absence shaped me in ways their presence never could.

Watching a man so full of life leave this world at only forty-two taught me an early and sobering truth: life is fragile and short, and none of us knows when our time will end. That loss trained me to move through life with urgency, to savor moments instead of postponing them, and to prioritize what truly matters: Love, Family, Fulfillment and the Present Moment.

The next major plot twist of my life arrived in 2018, when my thirteen-year marriage ended.

I met my ex-husband during orientation my freshman year at Adelphi University. He was tall, handsome, well-mannered, and easygoing, with a great sense of humor. What stood out most was that he did not seem bothered by my feisty, loud, and sometimes borderline obnoxious personality. Growing up, I was often made to feel like I was "too much," so I gave him extra credit for accepting me as I was.

What I did not understand then was one of the hidden costs of building an identity rooted in survival. It often comes with an intense need to be chosen even at the cost of self-betrayal. Many of my decisions, including choosing my ex-husband, were made from that place.

Although he had admirable qualities, there were fundamental aspects of who he was that did not align with my core values. I recognized those misalignments early, but instead of slowing down and choosing differently for myself, I focused on being chosen instead and on checking the box my identity was desperate to check: find a good man and start a family. In doing so, I downplayed what my gut knew was off, ignored the red flags, and convinced myself that commitment would smooth over what already felt wrong.

Before I knew it, I was walking down the aisle, saying "I do," and making a lifetime commitment that, in hindsight, was never sustainable. Ironically, the very red flags I dismissed in the beginning became the exact reasons our marriage ended 13 years later.

As you can probably guess, the qualities I truly wanted in a man were the ones I saw in my dad, my first love. I wanted a provider with an entrepreneurial spirit. A man who would take me on dates the way I watched my father take my mother. Someone who would push me to be better, to do better, and to dream bigger. A man with a wide vision we could co-create together, just as I had witnessed with my parents.

Instead, I denied myself all of that in the name of playing it safe. I was afraid of getting hurt again. So I chose the man I believed would not abandon me. Then I spent the next thirteen years trying to turn my husband into the man I secretly wished he was. Spoiler alert: It never happened...

I overextended and overexerted myself. I carried too much of the marriage and wore myself down trying to hold everything together. Before long, resentment grew and the weight became too heavy, and I cracked and the marriage ended.

The dynamic was unnatural for who I was at my core, even for the strong woman I had embodied for so many years. Even she grew tired. Even she longed to be taken care of.

Here is the truth about patterns and unresolved trauma. If you do not face them, they follow you. As I said earlier, if you do not tend to your childhood wounds, your relationships will. And they sure did for me.

After my marriage ended, I entered another relationship that lasted six and a half years. It began with sparks flying. I was swept off my feet. But before long, the same unresolved patterns found their way into that relationship too. It was only after its cataclysmic ending that I was forced to take a hard, honest look at myself. At my wounds. At my patterns.

That was when I chose to heal. I chose to give myself the gift of my own wholeness.

This is the space from which I am writing this book. I am fully sold on the truth that every twist, every turn, worked together to bring me here. To this moment. To this message. To this mission.

I am not one to speak in theories. If I have not lived it, I do not consider myself qualified to speak on it. To write a book about getting off the clearance rack, I first had to know what it felt like to be on it. I had to learn what it takes to step off it and what it feels like to live off the clearance rack and in a priceless life.

I did not know I was on the clearance rack until I knew I was on the clearance rack... like a fish in water. A fish does not know it is in water until it is pulled out.

I remember it as clear as day, except it was not daytime. It was an October evening in 2017. The night it became clear to me that I was on the clearance rack. The night I decided I was done settling for less and resolved to take myself off it.

The day itself started like any other. I woke up early to get my then nine- and four-year-old ready for school. I made breakfast, packed lunches, dropped them off, and came back home to run my busy virtual personal injury law practice, along with a staffing agency I co-owned with a partner. Around 2:20 p.m., I stopped whatever I was doing to get in the pickup line at my kids 'school for their 2:30 dismissal. Once we were back home, I jumped right into cooking, managing the kids, and continuing to take calls and work my cases.

This had been my life for years, and honestly, I was happy. I loved the flexibility of working from home. I loved being a hands-on, present mother while building a solid legal practice and launching other business ventures. I loved it. I was a full-time mom, a full-time business owner and breadwinner.

What I did not love was that the lion's share of the household responsibilities fell on me by default, I guess because I worked from home. Although my then-husband lived in the house, he rarely volunteered to help. Unless I asked or specifically delegated chores to lighten my load, nothing happened.

By the time I was asking for help and assigning tasks, I was already frustrated, and yes, I was not nice. The more this pattern repeated, the more bitter I became. The more bitter I became, the less respect I had for him, and the sharper my tongue grew. On top of that, I had to ask for flowers, date nights, and quality time just to keep our marriage watered.

Date nights mattered deeply to me, but trying to make them part of our marriage felt impossible. I would ask, but he rarely planned anything. My ex-husband preferred watching basketball games and playing PlayStation over the connection I craved. At one point, I even suggested we take turns planning date nights. When it was my turn, the date happened. When it was his turn, well, nothing.

I felt like I had a roommate, not a husband. I felt unappreciated and, in some ways, abused. Not physically. Not mentally. It was an abuse of my effort. I felt like if he saw me carrying six tires around my neck and bend down to pick up a seventh, he would simply help me put the seventh tire around my neck.

The more I did, the more I was expected to do. Once, while watching me grow my law firm, he commented that as my business expanded, my contribution to the household should increase proportionately. The word he used was "pro-rata"... The buffoonery of it all. With the pace of my hustle, I was on my way to diluting his contribution to nothing.

That October evening, I had reached my limit.

I asked him to join me on the patio of the townhouse we shared. He closed the sliding door behind him and sat across from me. I told him I was tired of begging for acknowledgment and support. Tired of being treated like a roommate instead of a wife. Tired of always having to tell him what needed to be done.

This was not the first time I had said these things. As I listened to myself speak, it felt like I was replaying a recording of a conversation we had already had a hundred times. But this time, the conversation took a different turn.

I said something like, "Forget taking me out to dinner. At least one night a month, why can't you stop at Publix, pick up some chicken and a bottle of wine, give me the night off, and spend real time with me?"

He looked me straight in the eyes. I will never forget the sincerity in them. Calmly, plainly, he said, "I know these are the things you would like me to do for you, but it is not in my DNA to think about doing these things for you."

Those words.
His truth.
The truth.

In that moment, I knew my marriage was over.

I stood up, looked at him, and said, *"Well, it's not in my DNA to be with a man who doesn't have that in his DNA."* And just like that, I told him he had lost his wife and I walked away. I went upstairs to my room, my heart raw. Me, Kara, the woman, wife, and mother I knew I was. Eighteen years with this man, thirteen of them married, and he couldn't even get me some chicken from Publix for a simple date night at home? How did I get here? What did I miss? How did I spend so much of my life with someone who didn't even have that little bit in his DNA for me? At this point, I wasn't even on clearance anymore. This was Goodwill and Salvation Army status.

His honesty, sharp as it was, cut me deep, but it also set me free. Once his true feelings rolled off his tongue, I could never unhear them. Even as we tried counseling for the sake of the children, my heart remained closed to him. Hearing his truth brought instant finality. I was done. It was the end of expecting anything from him, the end of begging, pleading, and hoping. It was the end of disappointment. I had to swallow that bitter pill and remind myself that disappointment is just misplaced expectation. I had been expecting things from my husband that were never going to come. How much more misplaced could my expectations have been? And how had I missed his truth for so long? How deep was my denial?

The good thing is that once his truth hit my core, I *got it*. It was a *say less* moment. Losing hope felt freeing. When you accept the truth about a situation you've been denying, the loss of hope can be priceless. You see clearly that the change you were chasing isn't coming, and two choices appear: make peace with reality or move on. For me, there was no making peace with not being treated like the woman I knew I was. By that October evening, I had spent years working on myself. I became starkly aware of how deeply discounted I had been but also keenly aware of my worth. I was done settling for breadcrumbs. I wanted more for my love, my company, my vision, my aspirations, my growth, my partnership. And it was clear my husband couldn't or wouldn't give it. It was not in his DNA. Case closed.

Painful as it was, my divorce became the catalyst for the life I live today. Leaving that marriage was a gigantic step off the clearance rack. Since then, I've experienced more abundance, joy, and fulfillment than I ever imagined. I've created unforgettable memories with my children and afforded us the lifestyle I once hoped to build within my marriage. I remember the many voices urging me to stay for the kids. I left for them, and it stands as one of the best decisions I've ever made.

I will admit, though, after leaving my marriage, I made one mistake, which in hindsight wasn't a mistake at all. I jumped into another long-term relationship, six and a half years to be exact, without taking the time to heal, a decision that taught me a painful lesson: be careful who walks into your life when you're vibrating low... When my marriage ended, I was at my lowest, desperate for the love and attention I hadn't received in my marriage. That's when a salt-and-pepper-haired Greek with a sexy accent swept me off my feet. I ignored every red flag and jumped head first into the illusion I created in my mind for what I wanted him and this to be.

Without that relationship, I wouldn't have the wisdom I'm pouring into this book. Despite incredible experiences and a different setting, I soon found myself facing the same patterns: low effort, the bare minimum, feeling undervalued. More on that in the next chapter.

CHAPTER 3

HOW I GOT ON THE CLEARANCE RACK AND WHAT IT COST ME

"When you say 'yes' to others, make sure you are not saying 'no' to yourself. "

— Paulo Coelho

ooking back at my marriage and the long-term relationship that followed, I realized how clearly my own behaviors had contributed to putting myself on the clearance rack, accepting low effort, breadcrumbs, and half-hearted love. The patterns were obvious once my pink-colored lenses gave way to clear vision. As you read along, you might recognize some of these same behaviors in your own life, quietly leading you down the same path. Take heed.

One of the biggest patterns that kept me on the clearance rack was projecting my own depth, character, and potential onto other people, especially men. As I came to realize, I wasn't always in love with who they were as much as I was in love with who I believed they could become. I was in love with a made-up version of them that didn't exist. I took the best parts of myself, my loyalty, my resilience, my vision, my ability to grow, and projected them onto people who had never shown me, clearly or consistently, that they possessed them. I clung to potential instead of paying attention to their actions and patterns.

That illusion had me tolerating disrespect, inconsistency, emotional unavailability, and bare-minimum effort. I overstayed, waiting for the version of them that existed only in my imagination. Every time I overlooked what was actually happening in front of me, I quietly discounted myself. I made excuses for behavior that hurt me, rationalized red flags, and carried the emotional labor of the relationship as if it were my job description.

The harsh truth I had to face was this: they were never going to become the person I kept projecting onto them. The potential I saw in them was actually what I would do if I were in their shoes. But I am not in their shoes. They are. And the fantasy I created was just that, a fantasy. I was so committed to who I wished they could be that I made endless excuses for who they really were. Until my rose-colored glasses shattered against the truth, I was actively participating in my own discounting.

I also had a pattern of adapting to poor behavior instead of walking away when it fell below my standards. If I'm being honest, I wasn't clear on what my standards were. I kept shrinking my expectations to match what they were willing to give. I excused things that hurt me until I could barely hear my own truth beneath all the justification. I told myself I was being understanding, compassionate, or "ride or die," but in reality, I was abandoning myself in real time. Every time I swallowed my disappointment, ignored my intuition, or over-explained my needs to someone who had no intention of honoring them, I quietly moved further down the pricing ladder.

I accepted breadcrumbs, convincing myself that occasional effort, sporadic affection, or future promises were enough to stick around for. I treated the bare minimum as if it were a down payment on the love, respect, and commitment I hoped would eventually arrive.

What I learned the hard way is that crumbs never turn into a full meal, and inconsistency never turns into stability just because I stayed loyal. That's how I ended up on the clearance rack, not because anyone put me there, but because I kept negotiating against my own worth. I had to face the hard truth: I will never be enough for the wrong person, and the right person will not require me to contort or minimize myself. The moment I decided to stop adapting to dysfunction, stop explaining away bad behavior, and stop trying to turn crumbs into a feast was the moment I began walking myself off that rack and back into my full value. If this hit home for you, good. I feel you and you are exactly why I decided to write this book.

Another pattern that dragged me straight onto the clearance rack was my habit of saying *yes* when everything in me was screaming *no.* I did not just overextend my time, I overextended my spirit. I said yes to favors I did not have the capacity for, yes to conversations I was not emotionally available for, yes to second chances that were really just repeats of the same lesson. I treated my energy like it was limitless and my boundaries like they were optional. Beneath that habit lay a fear, a fear of rejection, abandonment, misunderstanding, or being labeled "difficult" if I dared to honor my limits. So I became agreeable at my own expense, performing emotional gymnastics to keep everyone comfortable except myself.

Every unnecessary *yes* quietly chipped away at my value. Every time I agreed to things that drained me, to relationships that no longer fit, to environments that did not align, I was betraying myself and teaching others to do the same. I showed people that they did not need to consider my needs, because I was not fully considering them either. That is how I ended up on the clearance rack, not overnight, but choice by choice, compromise by compromise, yes by yes.

And then there were the red flags I ignored. The very same red flags I overlooked at the start of my marriage, and again with the man I dated after my divorce, were the very reasons those relationships ended. I romanticized potential and downplayed patterns. Every time I explained the obvious away, I stepped further from self-respect and closer to a version of myself willing to tolerate almost anything just to avoid losing someone.

Those red flags were not challenges for me to conquer, they were signals meant to alert me to save myself. Instead, I leaned in, treating them like a challenge. I ignored my intuition repeatedly and stayed in situations that forced me to live in constant internal conflict, wrecking my nervous system in the process.

Staying on the clearance rack is a very costly proposition.

First, there's the *emotional cost.* At times, it felt like I was on a rollercoaster with dizzying highs and crushing lows. Other times, it was a low-grade, persistent ache that showed up as resentment, disappointment, anxiety, and even self-doubt. My nervous system stayed on edge, waiting for the next letdown or broken promise. Over time, I began to question my own perception, my worth, and even my sanity. This is the kind of emotional erosion that does not just hurt. It chips away at your identity, your confidence, and your ability to trust your own judgment.

Next is the *financial cost.* The clearance rack is very ironically expensive. Staying in relationships, jobs, or environments that drain you inevitably drains your resources as well. Your confidence fades, your self-worth diminishes, and quietly, almost invisibly, your ambition and vision are chipped away. You have less energy to invest in yourself or your dreams because you are over giving to people who do not replenish you or invest back. Sooner or later, this imbalance hits your bank account. You find yourself paying for things you have no business paying for while trying to prove worthiness that is not yours to prove. You are giving the entire bakery away in exchange for breadcrumbs, and that cost is steep.

I had one of my biggest financial years after walking away from my marriage. And as I type these words, I have just taken a financial hit from the relationship I recently left. It was not until I got on a call with my accountant and saw the numbers that I grasped the magnitude of the impact. It was both shocking and sobering. I do not want that for you. I do not want it for me. I do not want it for any woman. If this book helps even one woman step off the clearance rack faster than I did, then my pain, loss, and hard lessons will not have been in vain.

Every time you stay where you no longer belong, you pay. Period. Emotionally, financially, and through missed opportunities. While you are busy trying to fix, manage, or perform in spaces that do not value you, you forfeit the chance to be around people and environments that would nurture and invest in you naturally. You miss opportunities to collaborate, learn, pivot, and build because your energy is tied up just trying to survive. The sooner you leave toxic environments and relationships, the sooner you can step into spaces that *water you.*

I could go on about the costs of staying on the clearance rack, but I will highlight one more. Staying on the clearance rack distracts you from your *self-actualization.* To me, the highest cost is being kept from becoming who you are truly meant to be. When your energy is spent proving, explaining, fixing, or chasing validation, there is little left for purpose. Your dreams get pushed to the back burner. Your gifts lie dormant. Your calling is drowned out by the noise of situations and relationships beneath your assignment. Self-actualization requires clarity, courage, and space to hear yourself, honor your desires, and build what you are meant to create. Staying discounted keeps you in survival mode instead of creator mode. The real loss is not just what you do not achieve, but the version of you the world never fully meets, the one with incredible talents lying dormant because you are too depleted to nurture or express them.

As Nathaniel Branden says, *"The first step toward change is awareness. The second step is acceptance."* That's why I've included a QR code at the end of the book that gives you access to my Clearance Rack Assessment and Cost Worksheet. If you feel led to use it, I encourage you to complete it for yourself.

It's often the first and hardest step but once you see the truth, you can't unsee it and from that clarity, change begins to unfold naturally.

CHAPTER 4

THE NECESSARY GOODBYES

"When people show you who they are, believe them the first time."

— Maya Angelou

One of the hardest lessons of my thirties, one I wish I had learned sooner, is that people come into your life for a reason, a season, or a lifetime. The pain often comes from not knowing which is which. I spent years trying to make seasonal people permanent fixtures, holding on to connections that had already served their purpose. I kept myself on the clearance rack, mistaking comfort for compatibility, and history for destiny.

What I now understand is that everyone is a mirror, reflecting back the parts of ourselves we most need to see, heal, or release. Some souls are sent to wake you up, others to walk with you for a while, and a few rare ones to stay for life. But no matter how deeply you love, or how much you give, people can only meet you as deeply as they have met themselves. When you grasp that truth, you stop forcing what's fading. You begin to bless it for what it taught you and free yourself to make room for the ones aligned with your next level.

Trying to extract lifetime commitment from seasonal connections is like trying to grow an oak tree in a pot meant for herbs. You'll exhaust yourself, stunt your growth and still end up disappointed. I tried doing that with both my ex-husband and the relationship that followed, with friendships and even family. It doesn't work. It hurts, and it wastes your time. The wisdom is learning to honor each connection for what it is, receive the gift it came to bring, and release it with grace when its time has passed, rather than clinging to what was never meant to stay.

Remember that you cannot change people, no matter how convincing you are, no matter how many facts or evidence you present to persuade them. Change comes only when they want it, or perhaps when the pain of staying the same becomes greater than the pain of changing.

We often assume that others will love, communicate, or show up with the same heart, integrity, or awareness that we do, but that's not always the case. Everyone operates from their own level of healing, consciousness, and self-awareness. When you truly understand this, you stop taking their limitations personally. You stop trying to draw oceanic depth from a shallow well. Your standards reflect the work you've done on yourself, not a guarantee that others have done the same. So instead of lowering your standards to meet someone where they are, hold your frequency. Let them rise or release them with grace and love.

When this understanding becomes your belief, releasing people from your life, or loving them from a distance, hurts less. You come to understand, with empathy, that you cannot teach people to love you. If their capacity to love is not what you feel you deserve, you can choose a different path, one free of bitterness. What might once have felt devastating can now be met with acceptance, gratitude, and understanding.

I once read a quote by singer and songwriter Kelly Clarkson that said, *"Divorce is not a failure. It's a success. It's the success of realizing you deserve better."* And honestly, what could possibly be wrong with that?

There is nothing wrong with you, and there is nothing wrong with them. Sometimes, it is simply a graduation from a dynamic that has run its course. When you have learned all there is to learn to earn a degree and it is time to graduate college, it is celebrated. Yet when you have learned all there was to learn in a relationship and it is time to move on, a heavy stigma of failure is attached.

I overstayed in an unhappy marriage for five years trying to avoid that stigma. I did not want to fail at something I was not actually failing at. I was ascending. I was growing. And yet, it could not be celebrated because society has conditioned us to believe that divorce equals failure, quitting, or not trying hard enough. It took an immense amount of courage and a complete shift in mindset to go against what I once believed, what the people around me were saying, and what society insisted divorce meant.

What my experience showed me is that my divorce was one of the greatest power moves and truest successes of my life. While society told me I should stay for the kids, I embraced the truth that I needed to leave *for* my kids. I wanted more for them than I could ever give them inside that marriage. I wanted more for myself, and I wanted more for him, more than he wanted for himself.

I tried so hard to bring him along, to convince him to grow with me, to dream with me. By the end, the thought that echoed through every fiber of my being was simple and clear: *you can take a horse to water, but you cannot make it drink and you cannot take a thirsty horse with you.* I also realized that no one was coming to save me from that ending season of my life. I had to save myself and save myself I did.

The end of a relationship can be a beautiful completion of a successful season. A season that has simply fulfilled its purpose. It can be a powerful rebirth into a new chapter. It can be an invitation to authentic reinvention, or a realignment with your truest self. What is so wrong with that?

As I healed from the immense pain of my divorce, I realized that much of the suffering came from how I initially viewed it. The social lens I once lived through made me feel selfish for choosing myself, even though deep down I knew my children deserved a happier mother. It took living as a more joyful, grounded, abundant version of myself to finally embody the truth. My divorce was a success, and society was wrong.

It was not only a success for me, but a success for my children. I became better able to show up as my best self, and because of that, I could offer them a fuller, richer, more expansive life.

Since my divorce, my children and I have lived more than we ever did before. We have traveled and stayed in some of the most luxurious places we had ever known. I have taken them to Hawaii, Puerto Rico, the Dominican Republic, Bimini, Vail, New York, Los Angeles, the Cayman, Europe... We went to Wimbledon during our time in London, ate endless crêpes in Paris, and stood at the Vatican, seeing Pope Francis just months before he passed.

We have dined at Michelin-star restaurants, and I have exposed my children to the life I wish for them. What a tragedy it would have been if I had not pulled the trigger, if I had not found the courage to give myself a second chance and allow a new chapter to unfold.

I have done more living since my marriage ended than I have ever done during the entire duration of the marriage. And that, to me, is not failure. It is proof of what happens when you choose yourself.

I make it a point now to regularly audit the people I keep in my life to make sure we're still a fit because the truth is, some people who once rocked with you stop rocking with you as you grow. They are fine with you until your growth begins to mirror what they could be doing but are choosing not to do. That is when the energy shifts. Conversations feel strained. Support feels thin. Presence feels forced. And no, you did not imagine it. It happened, and it has nothing to do with you.

How people treat you has everything to do with them and nothing to do with you or your worth. Their words, actions, and energy are a reflection of their level of healing, awareness, and emotional capacity. Someone who has not learned how to love and value themselves cannot love or value you the way you deserve. When you truly understand this, something inside you settles. You stop internalizing other people's behavior as proof that something is wrong with you. Their inability to see your light does not make you less radiant. It simply exposes the limits of their own lens.

You cannot change people. Period. Dogs bark. Cats meow. Snakes bite. When people show you who they are, believe them. Trying to rewrite someone's character is one of the fastest ways to drain your energy and erode your self-respect. Your job is not to convince anyone to do better. Your job is to recognize when they will not. The moment you stop trying to mold people into who you wish they could be, you reclaim your power. Acceptance is not weakness. Acceptance is liberation. Because once you see someone clearly, you can finally make choices rooted in truth, not potential.

I had to learn the hard way to stop making excuses for people's harmful behavior. I had a PhD in excusing disrespect, inconsistency, and mistreatment in the name of *understanding*. That is self-betrayal dressed up as compassion. Taking people at face value does not make you cold. It makes you wise. You can hold empathy for someone's pain without tolerating their patterns. The most self-loving thing you can do is believe what people show you the first time and choose yourself accordingly.

I have officially retired from my role as Captain Save-a-Hoe. I am not a rehab center for the poorly behaved people I love. I have become particularly skilled at loving people from a distance. I have finally learned to put my advocacy skills to work for the one person I neglected for far too long. I have been a fierce advocate for my clients for many years, yet failed to advocate for my most important client. Me. That season is over. Not anymore.

Another lesson I wish I had learned sooner is this. You will never be good enough for the wrong people, and that is not a reflection of your value. I lost count of how many times I was labeled difficult or told I was asking for too much. What I eventually understood is that I was never asking for too much. I was simply asking the wrong people. The ones meant for you will never make you feel like you need to shrink, overexplain, or earn your place in their lives. They meet you with effort, not excuses.

Words are cheap. And yes, I had plenty of smoke blown up my a$$ with words over the years. The irony is not lost on me. I am a lawyer and I love words. They sound *sweet*, almost intoxicating, like honey poured into my ears. And yet, that sweetness has often been my downfall with people. I learned, sometimes painfully, that words alone are not proof of character. Action is. Action is the real currency of integrity. If you truly want to understand someone, watch their patterns, not their promises.

If I had to offer you one honest tip, it would be this: give people the time and space to show you who they are before you grant them access to your heart, your energy, or your peace. Let them earn it. Think of it as a probationary period. Everyone may deserve a chance, but not everyone deserves permanence. You are the gatekeeper of your own life, and not everyone should make it past the velvet rope.

Be the bouncer at the door of your peace. Observe how people move through your world, not just how they speak inside it. Do they honor your boundaries? Do their actions align with their words? Trust what repeats itself. Protecting your energy is not being cold or closed off. It is being wise enough to know that not everyone deserves *VIP access* to you.

One of the clearest tests of who belongs in your life is how people respond when you set boundaries. Watch closely. The ones who grow angry, offended, or distant when you begin to set them are often the very ones who benefited from you not having them. When you finally choose to honor yourself, to say no without guilt and yes without self-betrayal, you disrupt a dynamic that allowed others to take more than they ever gave.

Not everyone will celebrate that version of you. Some will label you *selfish*. Others will say you have *changed*. What they really mean is that you stopped abandoning yourself to preserve their comfort. And that shift, while necessary, can feel threatening to those who were never meant to stay.

The people meant to walk beside you, the ones who love you from a healthy and grounded place, will never be threatened by your boundaries. They may not always understand them, but they will respect them, because they respect *you*. Boundaries are not about pushing people away. They are about making room for relationships that are mutual, balanced, and rooted in truth.

Those who fall away are not losing you. They are losing access to a version of you who tolerated what your healed self no longer will. And that is not loss. That is *liberation.*

Here are the top 3 rules I now live by when deciding who should or should not have access to my life.

1. I listen to the pang" in my stomach

We have all felt it. That uneasy sensation that settles in your body when someone feels off, when something does not quite "sit well". Sometimes it comes from a subtle misalignment of values. Other times, it is simply an unspoken sense that the energy is wrong. That pang in your stomach is not anxiety. It is your intuition, gently but firmly speaking.

Your intuition is your built-in guidance system. It is your soul's intelligent way of nudging you toward what is meant for you and away from what is not. It does not shout. It does not beg. Yet it is consistently accurate. When you ignore it, life grows louder, heavier, and more disruptive until you are forced to listen. When you honor it, life begins to move with a natural ease and a grounded certainty that logic alone cannot offer.

Your intuition already knows what your conscious mind has not yet fully processed. Trusting it is an act of self-respect. I have paid a painfully high price, again and again, for dismissing that inner knowing. I am wiser now, more rooted, and I would not dare ignore it again. Like a muscle, the more I listen, the stronger it becomes. Each time you follow that quiet truth, you strengthen the bridge between who you are today and who you are becoming.

2. I Conduct periodic audits

I do a periodic audit of the people I keep in my life, paying special attention to those who entered my life when I was not at my best.

Everything is energy. We attract people and situations that mirror the frequency we carry within us. When your energy is low, when you are tired, wounded, or simply surviving because life is life-ing, certain people gain access to you who otherwise would not have aligned with your higher self.

I say this gently but honestly. Some connections that felt acceptable during your struggle may naturally fall apart during your healing. Many of the people who enter your life in your lowest seasons are aligned with your wounds, not your worth. Your light attracts many things. It attracts beauty and it also attracts moths.

As you elevate, as you heal, set boundaries, and remember your value, their access expires without effort. Do not panic. Do not cling. Do not try to hold on out of guilt or history. Doing so only makes the process heavier than it needs to be. As you rise, not everyone can rise with you.

Let this be both a caution and a comfort. Some goodbyes are sacred. They are not punishments or failures. They are evidence of growth. Do not grieve the loss. Honor the lesson. Each time you release what no longer matches your frequency, you create space for connections aligned with your next level of peace, power, and purpose.

3. The quiet exit, silence as your superpower

There comes a point in your evolution when explaining yourself and fighting for closure becomes exhausting and unnecessary. This is when silence turns sacred. The quiet exit is not rooted in avoidance or arrogance. It is rooted in preservation, self-trust, and peace. And believe me when I say this with loving certainty, peace is the real bag.

When you outgrow certain people, habits, or environments, words often fail to capture the depth of that disconnect. What you say is heard differently than you intend. You will drain yourself trying to explain your growth to someone who is committed to misunderstanding you, or who simply lacks the capacity to meet you where you now stand.

This is where silence becomes a graceful exit. A soft, dignified bow out. You do not need to justify your peace. You do not need to prove your growth. You do not need to convince anyone of your worth. In this context, silence is power. It is you choosing to redirect your energy inward rather than pouring it into explanations that will never be received.

The woman who learns to walk away quietly is a woman who trusts her inner knowing completely. Enforcing boundaries does not require noise. It requires calm conviction. You owe no one an explanation for protecting your mental, emotional, and spiritual health.

Those meant for your next level will honor your space, not demand your access. Silence creates room for clarity to rise and energy to reset. It is the pause where self-respect takes root. The quiet exit is not weakness. It is wisdom. It is the unspoken declaration that your peace is too valuable to be negotiated and that your next chapter does not need an audience to be real.

CHAPTER 5

HOW I GOT MYSELF OFF THE CLEARANCE RACK AND HOW YOU CAN TOO

"You alone are enough. You have nothing to prove to anybody."

— Maya Angelou

Getting off the clearance rack requires a deep level of humility and a painfully honest look in the mirror. Emotionally speaking, it is not easy work. I did not wake up one morning suddenly priceless. There was no magical moment, no grand announcement. I had to first admit, with a heavy but freeing heart, that no one actually put me on the clearance rack. I did.

I was the one who walked over there, lifted the hanger, and hung myself there. Every unnecessary discount I allowed, every "it's okay, don't worry about it," every time I shrank myself so someone else could feel tall and secure was another voluntary markdown on my worth. No one asked me to do that. No one demanded those discounts. I offered them freely, driven by unspoken fears: Fear of abandonment, fear of rejection, fear of not being chosen, not being enough, not being loved. You name it, I carried it.

Getting off the clearance rack began with one liberating and clarifying moment of honesty. I put myself here, which meant I could also take myself down. That realization was not rooted in blame. Emotionally, it was rooted in power. If I participated in my own devaluing, then I also had the authority to participate in my own rescue. That was the first internal shift. I could finally see that I'm the one who had been negotiating my worth the entire time and it was time for me to stop.

The way back began with falling in love with myself again. Not the polished, curated, social-media-ready version of me, but the raw, unedited woman standing in the mirror. I had to look at her with tenderness and start treating her like the love of my life. Because truthfully, she was and has always had been. I just did not know it.

Society had been conditioning me to search for the love of my life somewhere out there, as if love was a destination or a person meant to complete me. Meanwhile, she had been within me all along, quietly waiting for recognition. This truth is not just emotional. It is spiritual. It is even biblical.

Mark 12:31 (NIV) says, *"The second is this: 'Love your neighbor as yourself.' There is no commandment greater than these."*

We are commanded to love our neighbors, but the standard is how we love ourselves first. That means the first and most important responsibility is self-love. Not pride. Not arrogance. But honest, grounded, compassionate love for oneself. Only then can love flow outward to others in a healthy way.

Yet, so many of us have been doing it backward. I know I did. I tried to extract love from people, relationships, and external validation to fill the aching gaps in my self-worth. At the time, it did not sound absurd. It sounded necessary. It sounded logical when I was emotionally drowning in my own low self-worth soup. Only now, with clarity and compassion, can I see how deeply misplaced that search was.

Getting off the clearance rack began when I asked myself: *If I truly loved this woman, how would I speak to her?* How would I defend her when she felt small, attacked and under-minded? How would I advocate for her when she was tired, overwhelmed, or afraid? What would I want for her future? And just as important, what would I refuse to tolerate when it came to her heart, her time, and her well-being?

Self-love stopped being performative. It became stoic, grounded, and even a bit cut throat. It was no longer about bubble baths or temporary comfort. It was about operating from the knowing that I am exactly who I think I am, just the way I am, and just the way I am not. From that knowing came the courage to honor myself and to protect my boundaries without apology.

It meant self-validating my feelings instead of minimizing them when they told me I was overreacting. It meant ending the exhausting pattern of self-betrayal done in the name of keeping the peace with people I was afraid to lose if I spoke up. It meant going to bed on time so my body and mind could actually recover. It meant saying no to people who only reached out when they needed something, people who drained my precious energy yet never replenished it. It meant choosing environments where I did not have to audition, shrink, or perform to be accepted or to belong. It meant walking away from tables that no longer served respect or recognition. It meant loving toxic family members and long-standing friends from a distance, with compassion but also with firm self-protection.

Little by little, I began courting myself. I took myself on long walks and quiet dates. I listened to my own thoughts instead of drowning them out. I honored my needs, even when it felt uncomfortable, and I refused to abandon myself just to be chosen by someone who had not even chosen themselves. Slowly, the desperate need for external approval softened. In its place grew steady self-approval.

From that grounded place of self-approval came a stronger, more unapologetic level of self-love and self-advocacy. I began asking for what I knew I deserved, clearly and directly, and I stopped accepting breadcrumbs dressed up as effort. If it is not a *hell yes*, it is now a *hell no*. I no longer indulge in almosts or maybes. I want what I want, and I am no longer willing to settle for less than that.

Understand this: when you stop being available for disrespect, unrecognized emotional labor, and one-sided relationships, the entire ecosystem of your life begins to shift. People who were accustomed to feasting on your time, your empathy, your energy, and your talent without ever investing back will feel the change first. Some will push back. Some will attempt to guilt you or gaslight you. Many will quietly fade away. This is to be expected.

This is not proof that you are doing something wrong. It is confirmation that your boundaries are finally working. When you move yourself from the clearance rack to the top shelf, not everyone who once had easy access to you will be willing, or able, to rise to meet you.

You will have to make peace with watching people you once shared deep bonds with exit your life. At times, you may even have to choose complete silence to protect yourself from those who try to bait you back into your old, discounted patterns. You cannot become the full, priceless version of yourself while dragging along people who only knew how to love the diminished you.

There will be grief. There will be tender days when you miss the familiarity of old dynamics, even when you know they were unhealthy. There will be moments when loneliness tempts you to lower your standards, to reduce your worth, just to feel less alone.

In those moments, remember this. Every time you choose yourself, you send a clear signal to the world about how to treat you, and to life about what you are available for. Getting off the clearance rack is not a one-time decision. It is a daily practice of self-love, self-approval, self-advocacy, and boundary enforcement.

It is trusting that the people, opportunities, and experiences meant for the fully priced version of you will find you. And when they do, you will be ready. You will be standing tall, grounded, and clear, knowing that you were never actually on sale. You simply had not yet recognized your true value.

Getting off the clearance rack also meant *consciously* investing in myself and in my healing. It meant *intentionally* placing myself in environments that would stretch me, challenge me, and gently force me to look at myself. I had to form a different, higher image of myself *to myself*, and that shift felt necessary, even urgent. Growth no longer felt optional. It felt like survival.

I can still *vividly* remember the first big investment I made in myself. I was attending a three-day live event called the Millionaire Mind Intensive. Toward the end of the third day, the presenter introduced a higher-level success program. It included five live seminars, and my gut *immediately* aligned with it. I do not remember all the names, but two stayed with me. *Train the Trainer* and *Enlightened Warrior Training Camp*.

I already knew, *deeply and intuitively*, that transformational speaking and empowerment work were in my DNA, so *Train the Trainer* made perfect sense. *Enlightened Warrior* sounded interesting, almost mysterious. At the time, I had no idea it would become the most transformational experience of the entire program.

The presenter began stacking bonuses, slashing prices, and energetically building the offer until the total climbed to something close to sixty thousand dollars. I knew, *realistically,* that I could not afford that. So I whispered a quiet, desperate prayer. *God, please let them offer something I can actually manage.*

Then the price dropped to $9,997.

Before I could overthink it, before fear could fully talk me out of it, I was on my feet. Terror shot through my entire body. Every cell vibrated with panic and possibility. My knees cracked like old wooden floors under pressure. A loud, frantic voice screamed inside me, *Are you crazy? That is ten thousand dollars.*

I ignored it.

With shaking legs and a fierce resolve, I made my way to the back of the room. Fear was present, loud and relentless, but beneath it was something stronger. A decision. A promise to myself to change my life once and for all.

I walked up to the table and invested in myself.

I have never been the same since.

What I learned through those seminars, who I became- ten thousand dollars does not even come close to the value that returned to me. Had I not taken that leap, this book would not exist and neither would the version of me writing it now.

Tony Robbins once said, "You have to participate in your own rescue." That moment was mine.

You cannot expect someone else to come take you off the clearance rack. That is *your* job. Your responsibility. Your initiation into your next level.

On the morning of my thirty-sixth birthday, I boarded a flight to Fresno, California, to attend the second of the five seminars I had purchased, titled *The Enlightened Warrior Training Camp*. What unfolded there deserves its own chapter, but here is a brief glimpse.

For five full days, I lived completely off the grid. I bunked with a close-knit group of women and immersed myself in deliberate movement work, sacred ritual practices, and carefully guided exercises created to release pain, trauma, and long-buried fears. Each day stripped something away. Each night left me raw, reflective, and braver.

One of the most intense and physically demanding moments was the Inipi, a traditional sweat-lodge ceremony. Inside that suffocating heat, my body violently heaved as grief surfaced without warning. Painfully, my father's death rose first. Then my grandmother's passing. Then, heartbreakingly, the heavy darkness of a marriage that had been slowly draining the life out of me. It felt as though the parts of myself I had been dragging for years were, at last, ready to *be put to rest.*

The night before camp ended, we were instructed to walk across thirty feet of burning coal while holding in our minds the one thing we were prepared to release. When it was my turn, the answer arrived instantly, without hesitation or fear. My marriage. As I stepped onto the glowing path, I felt surprisingly calm. With each careful step across the fire, I grew lighter, freer, as if something deep within me had already let go.

I returned home from Fresno on September 14th. Exactly one week later, on September 21st, my ex-husband and I made the final, irrevocable decision to go our separate ways. It felt inevitable. The version of me who returned from Warrior Camp, the awakened, empowered, and unapologetically aligned woman, could no longer survive within the life I had outgrown. My mindset had shifted. My relationship with myself had changed and I no longer fit inside my old world.

CHAPTER 6

YOU ARE MORE POWERFUL
THAN YOU THINK

"You never know how strong you are until being strong is your only choice."

—Bob Marley

Life has a way of drawing out exactly what it needs from your character, often to prepare you for your calling and your purpose. When life demands strength, it does not merely test your limits. It pulls power from deep within you, power you did not even know existed. It places you squarely in the middle of circumstances that summon it from the very core of your being.

As I mentioned earlier, just two weeks after my ex-husband and I agreed to end our marriage, I met someone new. A charismatic businessman who, in many ways, reminded me of my late father. The chemistry was immediate, almost magnetic. The more I got to know him, the more I felt validated in my belief that better existed, someone who could truly see me. Our conversations were rich and profound, and for the first time in a long while, I felt like all my business insights and personal development knowledge were finally being received by someone who found them valuable and could use them.

He embodied so many qualities I had longed for in a partner and I felt like I could contribute the fullness of who I was with him. He was irresistibly attractive, handsome, foreign, with that undeniable silver-fox allure. It was not long before I was falling, deeply and completely. I felt alive, seen, and cherished. He awakened a side of me I had almost forgotten, a little girl finally noticed and adored. I wanted that relationship to work with every fiber of my being.

Yet, beneath the intoxicating charm and thrilling connection, there were glaring red flags, serious character-based warnings I consciously chose to ignore. The love bombing was just too intoxicating after the long drought of my marriage. Naturally, I eventually paid the price.

The real problem was that I had not done the necessary healing work after my divorce. I was so high on the ecstatic feelings he evoked that I found myself tolerating dynamics I should have fled from, compromising my worth once more. The packaging was different, but the underlying dynamics remained painfully familiar.

In hindsight, that relationship became a *deeply painful* yet *quietly transformative* lesson. Six and a half years in, I slowly realized I was entangled in a trauma bond, a narcissist empath dance, all rooted in the long unhealed wounds of my past. I was not weak for staying. I was wounded. It was only after the *cataclysmic, soul-level collapse* of that relationship that I was left with no place to run and no choice but to turn inward. I had to do the real work. The uncomfortable work. The somatic work. The integration of the fragmented, abandoned, and silenced parts of me.

That work, though excruciating at first, placed me squarely at the center of my true purpose. It clarified why I am here. It revealed my calling to *gently and reverently* hold space for other women as they walk their own healing paths. That heartbreak was so *brutally consuming* that it forced me to look at myself, my history, and my life through entirely new lenses. What felt like destruction was, in truth, initiation.

The real power shift came when I stopped asking, *"Why me?"* and began asking, *"What is this shaping me into?"* That single reframe moved me from victim to student, from sufferer to sculptor. Each time I courageously leaned into the pain instead of fleeing from it, I extracted another lesson. I stopped letting pain define me and began using it to *intentionally and boldly* author the next chapter of my story.

Your trials do not create your power. They reveal it. Your darkest hours, your most demanding seasons, your do-or-die moments are not designed to diminish you. They are meant to introduce you to yourself. The moment you accept that your challenges are not random punishments but purposeful assignments, everything begins to shift.

Consider this: If your next chapter requires courage, your current chapter will place fears directly in your path. If your destiny calls for leadership, your present will push you into moments where no one else steps forward. If your purpose demands deep compassion, you will walk through valleys that crack your heart wide open. These moments are not coincidences. They are *sacred, deliberate* appointments.

God does not give you anything you cannot carry. If the weight appeared in your story, it is because you were divinely equipped to lift it. The very challenges that once made you question your strength are, in truth, the proof of it. They were the chisels shaping the woman you are becoming, the central figure in your divine storyline. Every obstacle has served as both a test and a training ground for your next season.

The cross you are carrying is the precise weight required to build the spiritual, emotional, and mental muscles you will need for what lies ahead. The fact that this particular challenge found its way into your life means there is something within you waiting to be awakened. A dormant strength. An untapped wisdom. An undeveloped resilience. These qualities could only rise through this exact experience.

That breakup, as devastating as it was, became my *sacred, undeniable* phoenix-rising moment.

When you embrace the truth that you are being *prepared*, not punished, something powerful shifts inside you. You stop wasting precious energy on resistance and begin, with deliberate courage, to channel it toward transformation. Think of a caterpillar in its chrysalis. That dark, confined space is not a prison. It is a sacred incubator. The exhausting struggle to break free is the very process that gives the butterfly the strength to fly.

Your current season, no matter how painfully constricting or emotionally heavy it feels, is doing that same holy work within you. It is stretching you, shaping you, and strengthening you in ways comfort never could. And here is the liberating truth that can finally let you breathe again: the harder you are being pressed right now, the more expansive your next season will be. God is not placing obstacles in your way to stop you. He is offering intentional opportunities to grow you into someone who can faithfully carry bigger blessings, a broader platform, and a deeper, more meaningful purpose that is already waiting for you.

Power is not something you gather from the outside world. It is something you *remember* from within. You were born carrying it. Yet the relentless storms of life, the careless opinions of others, and the constant noise around you can slowly blur that knowing. Over time, they persuade you to forget who you truly are.

Still, every challenge, every so-called setback, arrives with purpose. Each one is a reminder that you are far stronger than you were ever taught to believe. You were not built to merely survive this life. You were intentionally, deliberately built for it. And when you begin to lean into that truth, something profound shifts inside you. Your inner energy softens, steadies, and then rises. You move from wounded reaction to conscious creation, from feeling powerless to standing firmly in your own becoming.

So stop shrinking back from your challenges. Begin leaning into them with conscious intention. Each time you face your pain, however uncomfortable or raw it feels, you are building tomorrow's version of yourself.

The main character never gets the easy path. She receives the transformative one. And that main character is you.

CHAPTER 7

HEAL YOURSELF SO YOU CAN FREE YOURSELF

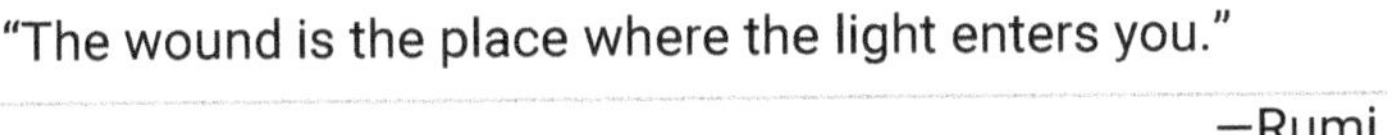

"The wound is the place where the light enters you."

—Rumi

I spent the better part of my adult life repeating the same patterns without even realizing it. Different relationships. Different people. Different environments. Yet somehow, the same story kept playing out. If this sounds familiar, that is again why I am writing this book. If what I'm about to share next only shortens your learning curve and process, then my mission was accomplished. To help you do that, I want to share something my therapist once shared with me, something that completely shifted how I saw my trauma and opened a wide, unexpected door to my healing.

I had been deeply triggered by something my boyfriend had done. My emotions felt loud, raw, and overwhelming. As I was recounting what had happened, she paused me and asked a simple question that changed everything.

"Who's talking right now?"

I stared at her, confused. "What do you mean, who's talking? It's me."

She gently followed with another question. "When was the first time you ever felt the way this made you feel?"

That question cracked something open inside me. In that moment, something painful and honest surfaced. I realized I was not one unified self making clear, conscious choices. I was a collection of fragmented parts, each carrying its own voice, its own wounds, and its own desperate agenda. The part of me that kept choosing emotionally unavailable partners was not the same part that longed for deep, safe intimacy. The part that sabotaged my success was not the same part that worked tirelessly toward my dreams. These parts were not flaws. They were remnants of old pain, frozen in time, still trying to protect me from dangers that no longer existed. In trying to keep me safe, they unknowingly recreated the very pain they were meant to prevent.

Understanding this fragmentation was profoundly liberating. For the first time, I began to recognize that at times, the six-year-old, the fourteen-year-old, or the twenty-one-year-old version of me was driving the car of my life, even though it looked like the adult version of me had her hands on the wheel. The part of me that stayed in toxic situations was the same part that learned early on that love meant enduring pain.

These were not conscious decisions. They were automatic, emotional responses from younger versions of myself who never had the safety or support to heal and grow up. They were still carrying fear in their small hands, still bracing for impact, still doing the best they could with what they knew.

Healing, I slowly discovered, was not about forcing myself to change or white-knuckling my way into better choices. It was not about shame, discipline, or self-punishment. Healing was about turning toward these fragmented parts with compassion. It was about listening to their fear, honoring their pain, and understanding where they came from. It was about gently inviting them back into the present, letting them know they were no longer alone, no longer in charge, and no longer unsafe.

As I began integrating these parts instead of fighting them, something shifted. I felt more grounded. More whole. More free. I was no longer living from my patterns but transcending them so I can step into what I really want instead of perpetuating experiences born out of childhood fears and pains.

Healing yourself is about *gently and intentionally* gathering those fragmented pieces of you and bringing them back into alignment. It is about *consciously and courageously* allowing the healed, whole, grounded version of you to take the lead, instead of the hurt version that is merely trying to survive. When you do this, you stop attracting chaos disguised as connection, and you begin choosing from clarity instead of conditioning. Healing is not about becoming someone new. It is about remembering the worthy, capable woman you have always been beneath the pain. The moment you begin this work, you stop replaying old stories and start writing new ones. That is where true freedom begins.

When you do the inner work, you begin to recognize the difference between chemistry and chaos, love and trauma bonding, comfort and calling. You stop trying to fix people and start focusing on the parts of you that tolerated what was never aligned. Healing is about *deliberately and compassionately* remembering who you were before the world taught you to forget your power. The moment you integrate those fragmented pieces, you stop being a magnet for pain and start becoming a match for peace. That is when freedom begins. Not by changing others, but by *fully and bravely* reclaiming every part of you that once felt undeserving of more.

Now let me be clear. Doing the work is not for the weak. You have to *willingly* lean into pain that most people spend their lives running from, just to reach the other side where most never arrive. But let me tell you why you want to be the one who did the work. Not doing the work is *incredibly* dangerous, and far more costly than you may realize.

If you do not address your childhood wounds, they will continue to live inside your relationships. Speaking from experience, the price is high. Not doing the work will cost you emotionally and financially, and it will also cost you opportunities, meaningful connections, and the richness of a full life. It will cost you time you could have invested in growth, projects you could have pursued, and healthy relationships you could have nurtured, if you were not still *unconsciously* entertaining chaotic and painful connections born from wounding rather than wholeness.

Use the QR code in the back of the book to access a worksheet that will help you assess the true cost to you. It is a sobering revelation, but it is also a necessary awakening. Once you see it for yourself, you cannot unsee it and there lies your power.

I don't mean to frighten you, but when you avoid the inner work, you become a target visible to predators, bottom feeders and parasites. For those people who survive on control, chaos, and emotional manipulation. The unhealed carry a signal. It is subtle, but it is readable. They can see your insecurities, your fear of abandonment and your deep need for validation. These things are then studied, mapped, and used as entry points into toxic dynamics that slowly drain your energy, your time, and your personal power.

The cost is not small. It is expensive and compounding. You can waste years of your precious life as the parts of you that were meant to be invested in growth, love, and stability end up trapped in survival mode instead. Healing is not a luxury. It is not optional. It is protection. It is prevention. It is the difference between attracting someone who feeds on your wounds and someone who deeply honors your worth.

When you refuse to do the work, you walk through life feeling broken. You resist the cards life has already placed in your hands. You live inside victimhood, emotionally limping, tender and exposed, feeling sorry for yourself while silently resenting the world. You spend years locked in a bitter standoff with reality, wishing your childhood had been softer, your parents had been healthier, your trauma had never happened, your losses had been avoided.

This resistance slowly becomes a low-grade war waged against your own life, and it is exhausting. You replay moments that ache. You try to erase pain that shaped you. You convince yourself that everything would be different if the hand had been better. But life does not shift because you fight it. Change begins when you choose the hand you were given as if it were the hand you wanted.

This is where *fully and deliberately* stepping into your main character role matters. You radically accept your life, and every complicated piece of it, as though it were the exact life you wanted and chose. The moment you decide to pick up the hand you were given and play it with intention, courage, and self-respect, everything changes. Your posture shifts. Your choices sharpen. Your power returns.

Choosing your hand means bravely taking ownership of your narrative. It is the powerful decision that says, "This is my story, and I will use every part of it to my advantage." This is where the sacred alchemy begins. Your heartbreaks transform into profound lessons and doorways to deeper awakening. Your traumas, once heavy and suffocating, become wise teachers. When you consciously choose your story, you stop seeing your past as a prison and begin to recognize it as preparation. You realize that the same cards that once felt unfair, even cruel, are the very ones equipping you for your next level of purpose and power. The magic was never in the cards themselves. It has always lived in the courageous willingness to play them boldly, intentionally, and with faith that nothing in your deck was ever a mistake.

This is also the season when the world begins to open to you in ways you never imagined. Opportunities arrive. The right people appear at the right time. Moments of divine alignment unfold with an almost uncanny precision. Life responds to your decision to stop resisting and start owning your path. Yet, while your world expands, not everyone around you will. Your growth will *inevitably* expose the places where others are still comfortable shrinking. It will challenge dynamics that once thrived on your self-doubt, your silence, and your smaller, more agreeable self. And this is where the next level of choosing begins. Because choosing your hand also means *intentionally* choosing yourself, even when it makes others uncomfortable and even when it requires releasing certain people.

The truth is, your healing and the elevation that follows will require separation. These are the necessary good-byes I spoke about in the previous chapter. When you begin walking in alignment with who you were created to be, not everyone will clap for your becoming. Some will question your change. Others will misunderstand your confidence. A few may even try to pull you back into the version of yourself that felt more familiar and less threatening to them. This is the moment when boundaries stop being optional and start becoming essential.

Aligning with who you were created to be naturally leads you to choose peace over people-pleasing. It means you will begin saying "no" to many things you once said "yes" to. Expect resistance. The people who benefited from your lack of boundaries will feel your growth as loss. They were comfortable when your "yes" came at the expense of your peace, when your compassion became self-abandonment, and when your silence protected their comfort. The moment you start choosing yourself, *firmly* saying "no," requiring reciprocity, and prioritizing your energy, you disrupt the unspoken agreements that kept dysfunction alive.

Their reaction is not proof that your boundaries are wrong. It is confirmation that they were necessary. Boundaries do not destroy healthy relationships. They reveal unhealthy ones. And remember this: "No" is a full sentence. You do not owe anyone an explanation for choosing yourself.

Also, you cannot heal in the very environment that broke you, no matter how fiercely you try or how much therapy you commit to while you are still standing in it. I learned this painfully, clinging to the hopeful belief that if I just worked on myself harder, meditated longer, set firmer boundaries, or practiced deeper self-care, I could somehow bloom in the same soil that poisoned me. But healing does not work that way.

You cannot grow into your fullness while surrounded by people who are invested in your smallness. People who relentlessly trigger your oldest wounds. People who remind you of the version of yourself you are courageously trying to evolve beyond. The truth, heavy and unavoidable, is that some environments are so toxic, so deeply steeped in old dynamics and painful patterns, that staying in them, regardless of how much inner work you do, becomes an act of self-betrayal. It is like trying to recover from a broken leg while someone keeps striking it, again and again, with a hammer.

The people, the places, the situations that broke you are not neutral ground. They are active participants in keeping you fractured. They need you to remain who you were, because your growth threatens the fragile balance of a sick system. Your healing disrupts what they have learned to control. Leaving is not giving up. Leaving is courageously giving yourself a fighting chance.

Isolation, though often misunderstood, brings elevation. Sometimes, loving people from a distance is the most compassionate choice you can make for everyone involved. This does not make you cold or unkind. It makes you self-aware, discerning, and wise. Distance creates the sacred space you need to hear your own voice again, to remember who you are beneath all the roles, masks, and adaptations you took on simply to survive.

When you step back from the chaos, the drama and the dysfunction, you finally meet yourself without all the noise. You get to ask yourself: Who am I when I am no longer managing other people's emotions? What do I truly want when I am not performing for an audience that will never be satisfied? What does my peace look like when I stop sacrificing it to keep others comfortable?

Loving people from a distance means you can still wish them well. You can still hold compassion for their struggles and acknowledge the layered complexity of your shared history. But you refuse, firmly and finally, to set yourself on fire to keep them warm. It means understanding that proximity is not proof of love, and that sometimes the greatest act of love is protecting your own healing by creating space between you and those who cannot, or will not, honor it.

Your elevation requires separation from anything that keeps pulling you back into old versions of yourself. And there is absolutely nothing wrong, selfish, or shameful about choosing you.

Prioritizing time with yourself is not selfish. It is essential and it is required. Because how can you possibly know what you deserve, what feels right, or what truly nourishes you if you have never spent real time in your own company? Solitude is where clarity forms. It is where you uncover your non-negotiables. It is where you separate what genuinely lights you up from what you were conditioned to accept. It is where you begin to hear the whisper of your intuition beneath the constant noise of other people's opinions and expectations. When you commit to time with yourself, journaling, reflecting, sitting with your thoughts, observing your patterns, something powerful happens. You begin to develop standards. Not shallow rules shaped by trends or pressure, but deep, soul-level standards rooted in your values and the life you are building. You learn that you need honesty more than excitement, consistency more than intensity, respect more than chemistry. These standards become your compass. Without them, you drift. You accept whatever comes and call it fate, even when it slowly drains you.

Once you truly know yourself and honor your standards, everything changes. You gain discernment. You gain the ability to choose, rather than hope to be chosen. Most of us have this backwards. We audition for others. We perform, prove, and twist ourselves into shapes we believe will make us lovable, all while neglecting the most important question of all: *Are you actually good for me?* Discernment asks you to pay attention early. In romantic, platonic, and professional relationships, you begin to look for character, consistency, and compatibility with the life you are building. You stop excusing red flags because someone is charming, because you are lonely, or because you fear appearing difficult. You observe how people respond when you say no. You notice how they handle your boundaries. You watch how they show up when things are inconvenient or uncomfortable.

And this is the part that shifts everything. You teach people how to treat you. Through your actions, your boundaries, and what you allow, you hand them the playbook. If you tolerate disrespect, you teach them disrespect is acceptable. If you abandon your needs to accommodate theirs, you teach them your needs do not matter. If you stay when you should leave, you teach them there are no consequences for hurting you. But when you know yourself and honor your standards, you send a different message. You teach people that access to you is a privilege, not a guarantee. It comes with responsibility. Those who truly value you will rise to meet that standard. Those who do not will quietly disqualify themselves. Either way, you win.

When you have worked on yourself, when you have *intentionally* spent that sacred, often uncomfortable time facing your wounds with quiet courage, and when you have *patiently* gathered those fragmented parts of you back into alignment, something subtle yet powerful begins to happen. You start to notice that the people entering your life feel different. They listen differently. They love differently. They meet you with a steadier presence.

This is not because you went searching for them, and it is not because luck finally found you. It happens because you now attract people who are a true vibrational match to where you *are*, not where you pretend to be, and not where you are trying to perform your way into. Energy is honest. It responds to truth, not effort.

When you were operating from unhealed trauma, from quietly stored fear, from emotional scarcity, and from wounded parts that were still running the show, you naturally called in people who mirrored that same frequency. The emotionally unavailable. The ones who took more than they gave. The ones who reflected back your own unfinished healing and longing for wholeness. This was not punishment. It was information.

But when you heal, when you *consciously* raise your vibration by doing your inner work and *gently* aligning with your truth, something remarkable happens. You become a magnet for people who are also doing their work. People who value growth. People who show up with integrity, emotional presence, and awareness. They meet you with the same grounded energy and conscious intention you have carefully cultivated within yourself.

If you pause and look at your outer world and feel uneasy about what you see, the recurring drama, the emotional chaos, the relationships that continually drain you, know this with compassion: It is not a failure, It's just a reflection. It shows you where healing is still asking for your attention. It reveals where old patterns are still active and where your vibration may still be tuned to frequencies that no longer serve who you are becoming.

And here is the *empowering* truth: You have the power to change this.

Heal, *intentionally*. Raise your vibration with honesty and self-respect. Then watch as your world begins to reorganize itself around the new frequency you are emanating. The right people do not appear because you have perfected yourself. They appear because you have *finally, courageously, and authentically* become yourself.

Suddenly, what no longer serves you leaves your life effortlessly, and witnessing it can feel both liberating and unsettling. You don't have to force the difficult conversation, draft the breakup text, or summon the courage to walk away because the universe does it for you. That friend who always made everything about herself suddenly stops calling. That relationship that drained your spirit slowly dissolves on its own. That job that suffocated your energy either releases you or you naturally drift away, free of the usual guilt or fear.

It is not magic, it is *energy*. When you shift your frequency through healing, you literally become incompatible with people, places, and situations that vibrate lower than you do. What once felt familiar now feels strange. What you used to tolerate now feels intolerable. The drama that used to pull you in now repels you. And here is the subtle, almost miraculous truth: the people and situations that are not meant for your renewed self sense this shift too, often before you even speak. They feel that they can no longer manipulate you, that you are unavailable for the old patterns, that something fundamental has changed. And instead of adjusting to your new frequency, they fade away, making room for what is genuinely aligned with who you are becoming.

Trust this process. When things fall apart after your healing, it is not a sign that something is wrong; it is a sign that everything is finally, beautifully falling into place.

A vital part of healing is cultivating a real, personal relationship with God, not the fearful one you were taught, but the one you can feel in your bones. Cultivating your connection with God means creating space for stillness, for prayer, for listening, not just asking. It is allowing Him to be your guide, your anchor, your confidant. When you invite Him into your healing, your plans take on purpose, your pain makes sense, and your steps are ordered in ways your logic could never have orchestrated.

Healing is not merely about finding yourself. It is about finding your way back to the Source that created you. And once you strengthen that connection, you no longer chase peace, you live in it.

Know this, no one is coming to save you. We grow up waiting for a hero, a partner, a mentor, a miracle, someone or something that will swoop in and rewrite the story for us. But here is the real plot twist, the rescue is yours to lead. Your healing, your growth, your freedom, your success, it rests squarely in your hands. Life will hand you tools, signs, helpers, and opportunities, but it will not carry you across the finish line. That is your job. You are both the rescuer and the rescued, the one who falls and the one who lifts, the author of your own remarkable story.

CHAPTER 8

THE POWER OF YOUR SUBCONSCIOUS MIND

"The mind is everything. What you think you become."

— Buddha

This is the part of the book where I take you through my journey of getting myself off the *literal* clearance rack. I first learned about the power of the subconscious mind when I stumbled upon Bob Proctor's *Paradigm Shift* video series around 2013. Until that moment, I honestly had no idea that my mind had two distinct parts, the conscious and the subconscious and that my subconscious mind was silently shaping the results I was experiencing in my life. That realization felt as though someone had handed me the keys to the Kingdom. It was so deeply life-altering that I could not keep it to myself. It stirred something inside me, a sense of responsibility, even urgency. I felt compelled to share what I had learned. That is what inspired me to write and publish my first book, *28,000 Days: Make Yours Count*, back in 2016.

For the very first time, I could understand why I kept repeating certain patterns, especially financially, even though I was *earnestly* trying to do better. I could finally see why, no matter how hard I worked or how determined I felt, the cycle of not enough kept reoccuring, literally keeping me on the clearance rack. Subconscious programming is not something you can overpower with sheer will. You cannot fight it from the surface. Real change only happens when you reprogram what is running beneath it.

As Bob Proctor explained it, the conscious mind is the thinking and reasoning part of us. It is the place where we analyze, decide, accept or reject ideas, and experience the world through our five senses. It is active, alert, and visible. He described it as the tip of the iceberg. Important, yes, but relatively small.

The subconscious mind, on the other hand, is the vast and unseen part beneath the surface. It stores our habits, beliefs, memories, emotional reactions, and deeply rooted programming. Much of it is absorbed early in life and reinforced through repetition. In his *Paradigm Shift* series, Bob Proctor emphasized that the subconscious mind *cannot reject* what is impressed upon it. It simply accepts. Like a recording device or a fertile garden, it takes in whatever is planted, whether helpful or harmful, whether intentional or accidental.

Those planted ideas eventually express themselves as behavior, recurring patterns, and results. They bear fruit after their kind. When you begin to understand the relationship between the conscious mind, what you choose in the moment, and the subconscious mind, what you repeatedly allow, something powerful happens. You start to see, perhaps for the first time, how your inner world is actively creating your outer reality and that realization changes everything. Because once you understand this dynamic, you also understand this truth. True transformation does not begin with force or struggle. It begins with reprogramming what the subconscious believes to be true. It begins with shifting your paradigm.

My first paradigm shift was around money. It began with a simple trip to Ross, a discount clothing store here in South Florida, where I live. I was there to buy work clothes. Nothing flashy. Nothing indulgent. Just a handful of power dresses so I could look polished and professional when meeting with clients. I remember carefully selecting dresses priced between $39.99 and $59.99 each. They were not expensive by any stretch. This was not a shopping spree. It was a practical upgrade.

As I stood at the checkout counter, watching the clerk scan each item and seeing the total slowly climb on the register, a familiar, uneasy feeling crept into my body. My chest tightened. My hands grew slightly damp. A quiet panic whispered inside me as I wondered whether my card would go through.

Instinctively, I reached for my phone and opened my banking app, hoping to transfer money between accounts before the final total appeared. I wanted to spare myself the embarrassment of a declined card. But there was no reception in the store. The app refused to load. My breath shortened. I began sweating, tapping my phone again and again, pretending calm while my nerves screamed. When the app finally opened, I rushed the transfer and my card went through.

The clerk handed me my receipt and two plastic bags filled with the clothes I had just purchased. I thanked her, walked out of the store, and stopped just outside the entrance. That was when the weight of the moment hit me. I felt deeply unsettled, almost repulsed by what I had just experienced.

I spoke to myself out loud, firm and offended. "Girl! After all the hell you've been through in your life, after all the dues you paid, a whole lawyer and everything, and here you are, buying clothes for work, not for clubbing, and you are worried about whether your card will go through? Oh hell no! Something is *definitely* wrong here."

That was the exact moment I resolved, consciously and unapologetically, to figure out what was happening inside of me. I needed to understand what belief, what silent program, was creating this constant sense of *not enough* in my outer life. You can call it my "line in the sand" moment when it came to money.

Thankfully, I had already been exposed to Bob Proctor's Paradigm Shift video series. I understood then, with growing clarity, that a money program rooted in scarcity was running in the background of my mind and it was not serving me. In truth, it was limiting me. It was shrinking me. It was keeping me small

It was keeping me on the clearance rack.

Literally.

When I got home that day, I sat at my kitchen table and asked myself this honest question: "What program am I running around money?"

I reached for my journal and a pen and began to write, slowly and truthfully.

The first memory that surfaced felt tender and revealing. My parents relocated to Haiti when I was only six months old. My father was the sole breadwinner, carrying the full weight of providing for my mother, my sister, and me. They were both in their early twenties, still figuring life out themselves. I can almost picture those early conversations around the kitchen table, shaped by the constant theme of *not enough money to go around*.

Growing up in the most impoverished nation in the Western Hemisphere only reinforced that message. I was surrounded by poverty, scarcity, and lack on a daily basis. It seeped into my awareness, into my nervous system, into my sense of what life allowed. Looking back, it makes perfect sense. No matter how much money I earned or how much success I achieved later in life, I kept recreating *not enough* in my reality because the program that was running me was rooted in lack.

Right there at that same kitchen table, with clarity rising and resolve settling in, I made a conscious decision. I would override this old program that had been clipping my wings. I began listening to books like *The Science of Getting Rich* by Wallace D. Wattles and *the Power of the Subconscious Mind* by Joseph Murphy on repeat, along with the forty-five-minute rendition of *Think and Grow Rich* by Napoleon Hill, narrated by Earl Nightingale. Their words gradually seeped into the soil of my subconscious mind, retraining my mind away from scarcity thinking into a mindset rooted in abundance.

I took a deliberate break from shopping at Ross and intentionally placed myself in more luxurious environments. At first, it felt uncomfortable and even frightening. Still, I pushed myself to make purchases that scared me. Each purchase was an emotional act, a bold declaration. I was repeatedly sending a new message to my subconscious mind that I had abundance, that *more than enough* was already my reality. Slowly but surely, abundance and more than enough began to mirror back to me.

There was one affirmation I held onto with unwavering devotion, repeating it softly and constantly. *I am so happy and grateful now that I never worry about what things cost.*

Today, I genuinely do not worry about what things cost. That truth feels grounding and deeply affirming, especially when I remember who I was standing in line that day at the Ross checkout, anxious and uncertain.

To reprogram my subconscious mind away from scarcity and toward abundance, there were a few practices I had to implement consistently and with intention. I will share them with you in the next few paragraphs.

1. Auto-Suggestion

The repeated affirmation, *I am so happy and grateful now that I never worry about what things cost,* is a practice known as auto-suggestion. Auto-suggestion is the conscious, intentional feeding of your subconscious mind with carefully chosen thoughts, beliefs, and affirmations until they quietly become your new reality. When you are shifting paradigms, breaking deeply rooted mental patterns, and installing new ones, auto-suggestion becomes the emotional and psychological bridge between where you are and who you are becoming.

The subconscious mind does not know the difference between what is real and what is imagined. It quietly accepts whatever is repeated with emotion, belief, and conviction as truth. That is why speaking abundance, confidence, and worth into your life daily is not cliché. It is neurological reprogramming.

Through consistent auto-suggestion, you begin to soften and override limiting beliefs formed through past experiences, conditioning, and survival patterns. Your inner narrative starts to align with the outcomes you desire. This process places you back in control of the most powerful creative tool you possess: your mind. When your subconscious is trained to recognize success, ease, and possibility as normal, your behavior, energy, and results naturally rise to meet that standard. There is less force and more flow. Less struggle and more trust.

Affirmations are essential in both speaking and *seeing* your new reality into existence. Every word carries frequency, and when spoken with feeling and certainty, affirmations begin to rewire the mental scripts that have kept you stuck for far too long. The subconscious learns through repetition, so affirmations act as daily downloads, replacing fear-based programming with empowered beliefs. When you affirm, "I am worthy," "I am abundant," or "I am confident," you are not merely repeating words. You are reconditioning your inner world to recognize these truths as safe and familiar. Over time, these declarations soften the old self-image and rewrite it, allowing abundance, confidence, and success to feel natural instead of distant.

In the Appendix at the back of this book, I share the affirmations I recorded in my own voice and listened to day in and day out to reprogram my subconscious mind. At first, it felt unfamiliar, even a little strange. Yet one thing I know with utmost certainty is this: it works. I have auto-suggested myself away from many undesired patterns in my life, and I often find myself living inside what now feel like auto-suggested prayers. What once felt forced now feels divinely aligned.

2. Visualization

Visualization is the intentional mental rehearsal of the reality you desire to create. It is one of the most effective tools for reprogramming the subconscious mind and shifting deeply rooted paradigms. During periods of change, visualization becomes the emotional proof your subconscious needs to accept a new story before it appears in the physical world. The mind does not distinguish between what is vividly imagined and what is actually lived. It responds to both with the same emotional imprint.

When you consistently see yourself succeeding, speaking with confidence, living in abundance, and taking brave, aligned action, your subconscious begins wiring that identity as truth. I personally moved from scarcity into abundance by doing exactly this. Every destination I have traveled to over the past six years existed in my inner world long before it became real. I remember visualizing Greece repeatedly, seeing the vivid blue rooftops of the Santorini calderas in my mind's eye until I stood there in the summer of 2022, heart full and breathless.

The same is true for the lush green mountains of Hawaii. I experienced them again and again in my imagination while soaking in quiet bubble baths at home, holding space for possibility. Then, in the summer of 2023, I stood there in the flesh, surrounded by that same beauty, experiencing it alongside my children. What once lived only in my mind had faithfully followed me into my life.

Visualization is a powerful tool that aligns your emotions with your deepest desires. Once you have *emotionally felt* the outcome before it arrives, that feeling begins to pull new circumstances toward you. At first, it may feel like a simple mental exercise, but over time, it becomes something far more intimate and transformative. It becomes reprogramming.

Through visualization, you can deliberately and consciously construct an entirely new life around you. What you repeatedly and vividly picture becomes what you naturally pursue. Your thoughts begin to guide your actions without force. This is how your paradigm softly shifts from possibility into lived reality. What once felt distant slowly becomes familiar, reachable, and then real.

The repeated affirmations of your auto-suggestion, when paired with emotional and experiential visualization, form a deeply effective formula for reprogramming your subconscious mind. This is where the inner work becomes alive. When affirmations are combined with visualization, they turn into a two-way communication with your subconscious. You see it, you say it and eventually, you live it. What once lived only in your imagination begins to express itself through your choices, habits, and confidence.

3. Positive Expectation

Another essential tool in reprogramming your mind and shifting your paradigm is positive expectation. Positive expectation is the calm yet unwavering belief that things are always working out in your favor, even when there is no visible evidence yet. It is not blind optimism. It is a conscious, courageous decision to expect favorable outcomes, aligned opportunities, and divine timing, regardless of how your present reality appears.

During paradigm shifts, positive expectation becomes the emotional anchor that keeps your subconscious rooted in faith instead of fear. The subconscious mind naturally follows the path of least resistance. When you consistently expect things to work out, you gently train it to look for solutions, meaningful synchronicities, and reasons to keep moving forward.

This energetic posture subtly magnetizes people, ideas, and resources that match your dominant vibration of trust. Over time, positive expectation reshapes how you interpret challenges. What once felt like setbacks now reveal themselves as quiet setups for growth. You stop bracing for disappointment and begin preparing for expansion. That internal shift in expectation becomes the frequency that calls your next level toward you.

4. Faith

We cannot speak about positive expectation in the process of paradigm shifting without speaking about faith. Faith is the highest vibration of certainty. It is the deeply rooted knowing that what you desire is already yours, even when there is no external proof yet.

As you shift paradigms, faith becomes the steady anchor that holds you between the vision and its manifestation. The subconscious mind thrives on repetition and belief, and faith nourishes both. It gently silences doubt and gradually replaces fear with assurance. Each time you choose faith over fear, you reinforce a new internal program that quietly affirms, *I am supported, guided, and fully equipped.*

Faith activates the creative power of the subconscious because it commands focus. It keeps your energy directed toward what you want rather than what you fear. Even if your faith feels small, even if it is only the size of a mustard seed, it is enough. That faith, when nurtured, becomes focus. Focus becomes momentum and momentum becomes reality.

Faith does more than help you believe in what is possible. It rewires you to expect it, embody it, and move through life as though it is already unfolding. Within the paradigm of faith, miracles are not accidents. They are the natural outcome of a mind that gently but firmly refuses to entertain defeat.

5. Massive Aligned Action

Now, let us be honest and grounded. You can visualize endlessly and hold the most positive expectations imaginable, but *faith without works is dead* (James 2:14–26). To bring your desires into your lived, physical reality, massive aligned action is required.

Aligned action is the physical expression of a renewed mindset. It is how you prove to your subconscious that you are serious about the life you have been visualizing. During paradigm shifts, action becomes the bridge between your new belief and your new reality.

Not all action creates transformation. Only aligned action, rooted in intention and guided by intuition, produces evidence of a changed mind. Every conscious decision, courageous conversation, and self-honoring boundary reinforces the upgraded internal program you are installing. Because the subconscious learns best through experience, each aligned move strengthens confidence and shortens the distance between intention and manifestation.

Massive aligned action converts potential energy into visible results. Those results then become familiar. Familiar becomes normal. And what once felt extraordinary gradually becomes your new standard of living.

CHAPTER 9

DREAM BIG:
THE UNIVERSE ISN'T ON A BUDGET

"Whatever the mind of man can conceive and believe, it can achieve."

— Napoleon Hill

Your desires are possibilities seeking expression

In my first book, 28,000 Days... Make Yours Count!, I devoted an entire chapter to one powerful truth: your desires are nothing more than possibilities seeking expression. That one truth shifted the way I approached life and living. I began to see clearly, that the map for my life had already been placed within me, woven into the desires, leanings, and longings I experience. Those desires became my inner compass. Simply put, if you want it, you are meant to have it.

Every desire that rises within you is not random. It is a sacred signal, sent from the part of you that already knows what is possible. Desires are not idle wishes. They are living instructions from your higher self, whispering what you are here to create, to experience, and to become. They are guidance from the heavens. They are life itself seeking expression through you. The same loving intelligence that planted the vision has already prepared a way for its fulfillment. Your role is to trust that if it was placed in your heart, it already exists within the realm of your reality.

When you suppress or doubt your desires, you unknowingly block the very power designed to expand you. Yet when you honor them, when you courageously allow yourself to embrace what you want and believe that those desires were placed within you because they belong to you, something meaningful shifts. You step into a conscious, creative partnership with the Universe. Your desires become evidence of potential waiting to materialize, and your belief becomes the quiet permission slip that allows that potential to take form.

The moment you stop treating your desires as distant dreams and begin seeing them as divine assignments, you start to magnetize the people, resources, and opportunities aligned with them. What you desire is simply what life desires for you. And when you emotionally, wholeheartedly embrace those desires, you are saying a powerful "yes" to the expression of the possibilities already wrapped within them.

The moment a desire is born within you, its matching reality is born too. In human terms, what you want also wants you. What you want is not playing hard to get. It is patiently waiting for you to take aligned, honest action toward it. That idea, opportunity, relationship, or lifestyle that keeps calling your name already exists in energetic form, waiting for you to draw it into your 3D reality.

When your thoughts, emotions, and actions rise to meet the vibration of that desire, something subtle yet powerful happens. You and it begin to move toward each other naturally, almost effortlessly. This is why forcing, chasing, or doubting never works. You cannot attract what you secretly believe is beyond your reach. But when you firmly stand in your worth, knowing you are already a match for what you seek, life begins to rearrange itself to deliver it to you.

What you want wants you because it was made for you. Your desires are not random or accidental. They are evidence of what is meant for you. When you remember that what you want is also seeking you, the entire game changes. Instead of exhausting pursuit, you step into partnership with possibility, with trust, with life itself.

This is all reassuring news, but do you know what is even better news? The Universe is not on a budget. Most people dream within the tight limits of what they think they can afford, handle, or justify. But the Universe does not operate on scarcity or spreadsheets. It operates in vast, living abundance. Dreaming big is not about being unrealistic. It is about operating in harmony with the true nature of the Universe.

The more you ask for, the more you allow yourself to receive. The Universe is not rationing abundance. It is responding to belief. So when you play small, you are not being humble. You are standing in the way of the infinite supply available to you.

The Universe does not measure your worth by your past, your mistakes, or your bank account. It measures it by your willingness to receive. When you dream big, you stretch your capacity not only for money, but for love, impact, freedom, and deep joy. You declare to life, *I trust that the supply is endless, and I am open to it flowing through me.*

That is when the magic happens. The vision you hold becomes the vibration you send. The vibration you send faithfully calls everything aligned with it back to you. Remember this: limitation is man-made, but abundance is universal. So, stop budgeting your dreams. The Universe has already paid the invoice in full.

From this understanding, it only makes sense to dream as big as you can. Allow yourself to feel *all* of your desires in their full weight and beauty, knowing that they are not random or selfish. They are meant for you. The abundant Universe you live in, generous and limitless, with an unlimited budget already stamped with your name, is standing by, ready to meet you where your faith dares to go. The quiet truth is this: you must be willing to release the good in order to make room for the great.

Some of the most profound, trembling acts of faith in my life have come from releasing what was merely good, and often safe, to create space for what my heart knew could be greater. It is a frightening choice, deeply unsettling, yet absolutely necessary. My divorce and my recent breakup are two very real, very human examples of choosing to let go of what was "good" so I could give myself an honest chance at experiencing something truly great. Those decisions were not careless. They were deliberate, painful, and rooted in self-trust and faith.

Comfort can be the quiet enemy of elevation because it persuades you to settle for what feels familiar instead of reaching for what is possible. The good job, the good relationship, the good season can slowly become cages when your soul already knows it was meant for more. Letting go is not loss. It is a courageous declaration that you trust something greater is waiting on the other side of your obedience. Each time you choose expansion over comfort, you signal to the Universe that you are ready to carry a higher level of abundance, purpose, and fulfillment.

The truth is that greatness rarely coexists with what no longer challenges or stretches you. The woman you are becoming cannot thrive in the same environment that once satisfied your past self. To rise higher, you must be willing to release the attachments that keep you safe yet stagnant. Letting go is a graduation. It is a spiritual promotion. And yes, it is deeply uncomfortable, just as it is when a caterpillar breaks free from the cocoon to become a butterfly, or when a phoenix rises from its own ashes. Still, it is the necessary tunnel to all things great. The sacrifice of your old self, and of what once filled your life, makes space for a fuller, braver version of you, along with the greater replacements that naturally follow that version. Trust that every ending is an energetic clearing for a new beginning, never a punishment.

Feel the Fear and Do It Anyway

Fear is the mind's instinctive attempt to protect you from imagined danger, not real limitation. Most of what you fear will never happen. It is a projection, vivid and convincing, yet untrue. A looping mental movie of *what ifs* that almost never come to pass. That is why fear is called False Evidence Appearing Real. It is smoke and illusion, designed to keep you tethered to familiarity rather than aligned with fulfillment. Every next level of your life will require a new version of you, and that version is always waiting on the other side of fear. That is simply how growth works.

Courage is not the absence of fear. It is choosing to act while fear is still present, still loud, still convincing. The moment you move anyway, the illusion begins to dissolve, and you come face to face with a powerful realization. The only thing that ever stood in your way was a thought, and thoughts can be rewritten.

Fear is the final gatekeeper before every breakthrough, and no one is exempt from its gripping hold. It is a deeply human, self-preserving emotion built into every one of us. Fear exists to protect us, but it is also our responsibility to discern when it is genuinely warning us and when it is simply trying to keep us small. In those moments, we must deliberately and courageously choose to move through it if we want the life we long for.

Every major win, every defining chapter of transformation, begins with one brave decision to act despite the fear. You do not need perfect confidence. You only need *just enough* courage to take the next step. And once you cross to the other side, it truly does get better. When you face fear head-on, life slowly, generously begins to open in ways you once only imagined. Every risk becomes a doorway to a higher level of becoming. The best days of your life are not behind you. They are waiting for you to show up, claim them, and believe you are worthy of them.

The moment you stop negotiating with fear and start intentionally partnering with courage, everything ahead of you begins to expand, gently at first, then powerfully. And it keeps getting better from there.

Let me let you in on just a few of the things fear tried to stop me from doing. Thank God I did not listen.

1. Starting my Mary Kay business as a licensed attorney and walking away from the steady security of my associate paycheck

2. Starting my law firm with no business experience and only nine months of legal practice

3. Getting divorced

4. Buying luxury items and upgrading to luxury transportation

5. Enrolling my children in schools with annual tuition exceeding $30,000 per child

6. Walking away from the familiar comfort of a toxic, long-term relationship

7. Putting myself out there on social media as a business and personal development coach when everyone knew me only as an attorney

8. Promoting my *From Clearance to Priceless* retreat without knowing if anyone would sign up

And the list goes on.

I share this with you because every single one of these decisions required me to pull the trigger while afraid. The fear sat heavily in my belly until the action was complete. I stretched. I grew. I leveled up. And it only happened because I chose to do it afraid.

I am here to tell you this with honesty and care. If you are waiting for fear to disappear before you move, it will not happen. You will remain exactly where you are, quietly frustrated and deeply unfulfilled. Fear does not leave first. The fear only leaves *after* you jump.

CHAPTER 10

YOU GET 28,000 OUT HERE. HOW ARE YOU GOING TO MAKE THEM COUNT?

"In the end, it's not the years in your life that count, but the life in your years."

—Abraham Lincoln

We have taken a meaningful journey together so far. By now, you know this.

First, the desires of your heart are meant for you. They are not random wishes. They are real possibilities, quietly seeking expression through you.

Second, the Universe holds a blank check with your name on it, patiently waiting to fund your wildest, most honest dreams.

Third, you have the power to align your mind with what you desire. Your job is to focus, clearly and consistently, on what you want and then take aligned, inspired action so those desires can take form in the physical world.

Fourth, you can meet your fears through action and, by doing so, gain full access to what the Universe has been holding back for you.

Now, let me offer you another vital truth.

You only have about 28,000 days out here, journeying in this human body, having this human experience. One day, you will die. The average human lifespan is about 28,000 days, roughly 75 years. After that, you are out of here.

My dad only lived to 42.

So, with that sobering truth in mind, let me ask you this: How are you going to make whatever number of days you have left count?

You entered this world alone, and you will leave it the same way. Everything and everyone in between is temporary. The characters, the relationships you build, the roles you play, that's just a part of your story, not the story itself.

Too often, we become so attached to certain characters in our story that we forget we are the main character. We forget there is a bigger picture story unfolding and that we are on a journey made out of different seasons and those seasons are not destinations.

Every soul that crosses your path is a teacher, not a permanent fixture. Let them play their part. Learn the lesson. Then, with courage and grace, keep writing the pages of your story.

I overstayed in my marriage. I wasted valuable years of my life sitting in indecision. I was 36 when I finally pulled the trigger after years of being deeply unhappy. For what?

I have had countless, heart-heavy conversations with women standing on that same fence. One woman once told me, "What am I going to do about insurance?" And all I could think was this. *Your life is a pretty hefty price to trade for health insurance.*

Life is happening now. Every single day that passes is one of your 28,000. This is not a dress rehearsal. We are live. Right now. Do not waste your days replaying chapters that are already complete.

The real gift of life is not time itself, but what you choose to do with whatever time you have left.

As we have already seen together, you had no control over how your origin story unfolded. You were cast into this role without consent, and here you are. In the same way, you cannot control exactly how your life will unfold next.

Yes, through visualization, you can call your desires forward. You can pull into your physical reality what has already been planted inside you. But the real work is releasing control over *how* those desires arrive.

Control, I have come to learn, is a complete illusion anyway.

The exhausting need to manage every outcome, predict every turn, and hold everyone and everything in place creates anxiety, tension, and emotional fatigue. It is also an impossible task. Life was never meant to be micromanaged. It was meant to be experienced.

The experience, however, is something you can choose. One of the most powerful ways to choose your experience is through surrender.

Surrender is the shift from forcing to flowing, from gripping to allowing. It is the realization that the Universe has always been conspiring in your favor and does not need your help to do its job.

So much of the unnecessary pain we carry comes from resisting what is already happening. We suffer not because life is cruel, but because we refuse to accept its rhythm.

The truth is, life moves in divine order. Sometimes messy. Sometimes miraculous. Always meaningful.

When you surrender, you stop fighting the current and begin floating with it. You realize that you were never holding it all together. You were also never making it happen.

And from that place of trust, openness, and release, everything becomes possible.

With only *28,000 days* in this human experience, you owe it to yourself to live the fullest, boldest, and most deeply aligned life possible. That means *truly* honoring your circumstances, your calling, your lessons, your desires, and the vision that keeps tugging at you, whispering insistently that there is more. And the only real way to do that is to mind your own business. Seriously...

the business of your life is the *only* business that, when tended to with careful attention, yields fruits that are entirely yours to have and to hold.

Staying in your lane isn't just a cute phrase; it's a profound cheat code for purpose-driven people. Every moment spent peeking at someone else's path pulls you away from your own. You are not going where they are going, and they are not going where you are going. Comparison is not only the thief of joy but of the very essence of your destiny.

As you move forward on your 28,000 days, be uncompromisingly discerning about whose voices you let echo in your life. Advice is cheap; alignment is priceless. Unless someone has walked the exact road you are trying to walk, taking their guidance is not just unhelpful, it is *dangerously* irresponsible. People project their fears, limits, insecurities, and unrealized dreams onto others constantly. Guard your mind like it is the vault to your future, because it truly is. The wrong voice can delay you for years; the right one can accelerate you in minutes.

And when you share your ideas, your dreams, or your plans and someone shuts them down, remember this: it's not because your ideas aren't worthy, it's because they are not *theirs*, and it is not their business. Why do you seek validation for something that is meant for *you* and no one else? People are, by nature, self-centered and protective of their own space. There is nothing wrong with that. They are minding their own business. You are simply expecting them to mind *yours*, and then you get offended when they don't. Can you see the absurdity in that? Just because you can get genuinely excited for others and make space for everyone, including yourself, does not mean that everyone else has the capacity to do the same.

It is your responsibility to take brave chances on your ideas during your 28,000 days. Life is your vivid, unpredictable playground, and you get only one ticket in. Try the things that scare you, jump before you feel ready, fail fast, fail big, and fail forward. Why play small when the ultimate end is the same for all of us, we will die anyway? Take the shot. Make the ask. Show up messy and be seen imperfectly. The only people who will reject you were never your people to begin with.

There are eight billion humans on this planet. Align yourself with the ones who align with you, the ones who like you just the way you are, who already understand you, who vibrate on the same frequency as you. Stop auditioning for rooms that reject you or were never meant for you. You will never be enough for the wrong people, and you are not asking for too much. You are simply asking from the wrong people. The people who truly want you in their lives will put in the necessary effort to keep you there.

And one more thing, practice the art of giving zero f*cks. Yes, I mean it. Stop obsessing over what people think, how they might react, or how you will be perceived. Who really cares? Let people hold their opinions while you stay busy living your life out loud. Be the woman in the arena, playing fully and fiercely, while the critics, the naysayers, the spectators, and the commentators, who are not even in the game, have their thoughts. They are not building anything; they are merely opining. People's expectations of you are none of your business.

Everyone in the arena is taking bold bets on themselves, and none of them know exactly what they are doing. But guess what?, they are in the arena figuring it out. They are taking shots. Some shots are hits and some are misses. The trick is to stay in the arena even when you're missing because the victories are just on the other side of those misses if you stick around long enough. So step into the arena. Keep shooting your shots. Keep daring. Keep living.

CHAPTER 11

CONCLUSION

"We must be willing to let go of the life we planned so as to have the life that is waiting for us."

—Joseph Campbell

As we reach the end of this journey together, I want to ask you something: Have you been wishing that life had been different for you? And if your answer is yes, who told you it was supposed to be different? Were you truly broken by your circumstances, or have you simply been living through the origin story of the main character in your life?

Can you consider the fact that what you once called "broken" was simply a period of profound character development, quietly unfolding without your awareness? The parents you were given, the heartbreaks, the losses, the victories, the unexpected plot twists- they have been happening *for* you all along. Everything was carefully shaping and molding you. The cracks you tried desperately to hide were actually the places where truth was trying to shine through. All those moments when you thought, *"What is wrong with me? Why do I keep ending up here?"* were invitations to remember the essence of who you truly are. They were reminders that the person you were trained to be, the one who pleases, shrinks, overgives, and overexplains, was never the fullest expression of your real self. The story was never about your brokenness. It was always about your becoming.

If you are a recovering control freak like me, this shift might feel unsettling, even uncomfortable, but indulge me for a moment. Take a pen and write down five to ten things you once desperately tried to control. Anything, anyone, any outcome. Then ask yourself: How did that actually work out? The wasted energy, the timelines you forced, the expectations you placed on people who were never meant to meet them, the inevitable disappointment that followed, all of it came from the same illusion, the belief that you were ever truly in control.

At some point, you must make a deliberate choice to release your grip on the future as if it were a steering wheel you could actually turn. You cannot control who stays, who leaves, who grows, or who refuses to grow. You cannot script people into roles they were never casted for. And truthfully, you have no clear idea what your future holds, or who is destined to walk into it. I certainly never imagined the details of the life I am living now, yet here I am, embracing it fully, deeply grateful and loving every bit of it. Life unfolds precisely as it is meant to, in the timing that is written for you. Forcing outcomes only exhausts you and delays the alignment that has been trying to reach you all along.

Your higher self already knows where you're going and who needs to enter or leave your life to get you there. So relax. Loosen your grip. Exhale. You're risking your peace trying to micromanage destiny. *Breathe... you're in good hands.*

Most of the suffering we feel is born from the illusion of control. Looking back, I see that much of my pain came from disappointment—things not going the way I imagined or people not acting as I expected, as if the ideals in my mind were promises. When my marriage ended, I wept over the life I had hoped to give my children: a life with both parents present, like the one I had known. I was so bitterly angry at my ex for not doing the simple things I thought would have saved our marriage. All that pain was because life didn't follow my script. That was it. I had misplaced my expectations, and when reality failed to meet them, I suffered. I had created a scenario in my head and invested in it, and when it collapsed, I ached. Sounds insane, doesn't it? But isn't that exactly what we do?

Your life is exactly as it is meant to be, just not according to your plans. What if this entire journey has been your origin story, the part of the movie where the main character still doesn't know she's the main character? Every person you met, every disappointment, every red flag you ignored, every "yes" you reluctantly said when you truly meant "no," every night you cried yourself to sleep, wondering if this was all life had to offer... what if they were all scenes in the script of your awakening?

The people who mishandled you were not proof of your unworthiness. They were mirrors reflecting the places where you still needed to choose yourself. The situations that stretched you were not punishments. They were training grounds. You were being prepared, refined, and revealed, not diminished. *You were being guided toward your becoming.*

When you look back through that lens, nothing was ever truly wasted. The time, the tears, the detours, the long seasons you spent feeling overlooked or cast aside, they all left you with receipts. Receipts in the form of hard-won wisdom, careful discernment, unwavering standards, tender empathy, unshakable resilience, and a richer, more intimate relationship with yourself. You learned to trust your intuition. You discovered what you will no longer tolerate. You realized that peace is non-negotiable and that your worth is never up for debate. Those lessons are not consolation prizes; they are tools. They are the very things that now equip you to walk boldly in your full power, to love with clarity, to lead with integrity, and to craft a life that mirrors your true value. Your purpose is woven from the pain you had to endure and the obstacles you had to overcome.

So this is where we land: nothing was lost, and from here, everything is possible. You are no longer required to live as the version of yourself that settled, performed, or begged for a seat at tables too small for your greatness. From this moment, you get to write your story as the main character, conscious, intentional, and priceless. The past is no longer a prison; it is a foundation. The patterns are no longer your identity; they are your testimony. You did not just lift yourself off the clearance rack; you built the courage, the clarity, and the consciousness to ensure you never put yourself there again.

Now, it is time to live with your hands open, letting people and opportunities flow freely through your life. With all that you have endured, all that you have learned, and all that you are, the next chapter is simple: you choose yourself. Fully, unapologetically, and on purpose.

ACKNOWLEDGMENTS

This book was born from a journey I never planned on taking, and yet it was the very journey I needed to shape me into the woman I was always meant to become. I want to take a moment to honor some remarkable people who walked this path with me, some more intimately than others, but all playing essential, life-shaping roles. The truth is, no one becomes whole alone.

First and foremost, my deepest gratitude goes to God. For it is through His design and this extraordinary path that I've come to understand my calling. This book exists because of the purpose He has woven into my life and the journey He has led me on. I am profoundly thankful for the chance to share this message and to be of service to so many women on their own paths.

To my sister, Erika, whose steady presence in my life is both grounding and uplifting: thank you for being my constant, my unwavering clarity, and my gentle reminder that I have never walked this path alone. Your love remains my safe haven- a place I can rest, be seen and know that I am loved unconditionally. Thank you.

To my brother, Joey, thank you for loving me so openly and purely. You are the kindest, most fun, and endlessly inspiring brother a girl could ever ask for, and the most incredible uncle to my children. More than anything, thank you for your friendship. You are the real deal, through and through, and I am deeply grateful that we get to share this life together. I love being your tennis rival—it brings me so much joy to kick your butt on the court.

I have been abundantly blessed with the most loving family. That Vaval Family love is one of the greatest gifts of my life. Thank you to my uncles, cousins, nieces, and nephews. You fill me with endless streams of love and unwavering support, and I cherish every bit of it.

To the friends who stood steadfastly beside me during the most tender, vulnerable seasons of my healing: thank you for holding a nonjudgmental, loving space where I could simply be and evolve at my pace. Thank you for your priceless listening as I repeated the same story a thousand times until I reached my breakthrough. Tanya, Ira, and Anique, the greatest gifts to emerge from my Mary Kay starter kit, your presence, your unwavering belief, your honest reflections, and your gentle encouragement were the scaffolding that kept me steady while I painstakingly rebuilt myself from the inside out.

To my book coach, Sandra, whose brilliance and structure facilitated the birth of this project I have nurtured for nearly seven years: thank you. There were at least five previous versions of this book, each evolving alongside my own healing. Over time, I realized that if I kept rewriting to match the next version of myself, this book would never reach the world. Sandra, your guidance, patience, and protective container allowed my message to do exactly what it was meant to do, impact lives. This book exists because you helped me step out of my own way and onto the page.

To my other coaches who poured wisdom, guidance, and encouragement into me throughout my evolution, most notably Mina Shah, Sean Smith and Lisa Nichols, you were sanctuaries of truth and safety. You gave me the space to confront every facet of myself, even the parts I feared most. Through your intentional calls, seminars, and retreats, I discovered my essence and reclaimed my voice. A deeply heartfelt thank you to Lisa Nichols, who blessed this project and wrote its foreword. Your life continues to remind me of what radical self-belief looks like in action.

And finally, to the unexpected teachers, the ones who arrived as "villains" yet became the profound catalysts for my growth: thank you. Your choices pushed me back into my own arms. You compelled me to meet myself, heal myself, and fight for myself. Without the contrast your presence created, I may never have discovered my power, my boundaries, or the invaluable version of myself I was always meant to rise into.

Every person, every moment, every wound, and every breakthrough was part of the divine architecture of this book. Nothing was wasted. Everything was preparation. Thank you.

THANK YOU

To my Reader,

Thank you for taking this journey with me. Out of all the books you could have picked up, you chose this one, and that means more than you may realize. The pages you just read were not written from theory, but from lived experience — the highs, the heartbreaks, the healing, and the powerful realization that none of it was wasted. If my story helped you see your own life through a new lens, then every moment that led me here was worth it. My deepest hope is that somewhere along these pages you recognized a piece of yourself and remembered something that may have been buried for far too long: your worth was never meant to be negotiated.

As you close this book, I want to leave you with a charge. Do not return to the clearance rack of your life. The world does not benefit from a watered-down version of who you are. Reclaim your voice. Reclaim your standards. Reclaim the dreams you may have set aside for far too long now. Your life is not meant to be lived as a supporting role in someone else's story. It is time for you to step fully into your Main *Kara*cter™ era, where you choose your path with intention, surround yourself with people who honor your value, and create a life that reflects the priceless woman you truly are.

Scan Me for access to the From Clearance to Priceless
Assessment and Cost Worksheets

ABOUT THE AUTHOR

Kara Vaval, Esq. is an attorney, keynote speaker, author, and transformational coach devoted to helping women reclaim their power, rebuild their confidence, and rise fully into the expression of who they were always m eant to be. As the CEO of The InPowerment Institute, LLC, Kara blends mindset reprogramming, emotional healing, and practical personal development to guide high-achieving women toward financial independence, inner freedom, and lives intentionally designed rather than passively inherited. Her mission is deeply personal, forged from lived experience, hard-earned breakthroughs, and an unwavering belief that every woman can rewrite her own story, starting with the narrative she tells herself.

Known for her candid honesty, infectious humor, and profoundly relatable storytelling, Kara draws from a life marked by trauma, heartbreak, reinvention, and eventual triumph. She transformed her wounds into wisdom, her setbacks into strategy, and her healing into a blueprint for others. Through her acclaimed courses, retreats, and coaching programs including the *From Clearance to Priceless*™ retreat, her *Main Karacter*™ brand and signature program, and her confidence and money mindset teachings, Kara has guided countless women through the inner work necessary to break cycles, dissolve limiting beliefs, and step boldly into the main character role of their lives. She also hosts two podcasts, The *Unfiltered with Kara Vaval* podcast and The *Laptop Lifestyle Lawyer* podcast, blending empowerment, personal truth, and business strategy to inspire a global audience.

Beyond her coaching and speaking, Kara is a seasoned personal injury attorney and the creator of *The Laptop Lifestyle Lawyer*® brand, a platform that helps women lawyers build profitable practices while reclaiming their time, money, and lifestyle freedom. Her legal expertise, entrepreneurial insight, and spiritual depth give her a uniquely holistic perspective on success and self-mastery. Kara's work embodies one enduring truth: you are never truly starting over; you are simply stepping into the version of yourself you were always being prepared to become. She is here to show women everywhere how to rise from clearance to priceless.

Kara is also a devoted mother to her two incredible children, Luc and Lia, her constant inspiration, her deepest why, and the joy that fuels everything she does.

ABOUT THE PUBLISHER

At **Soulful Books**, we believe in the power of storytelling to heal, inspire, and create lasting impact. Founded by best-selling author **Sandra Rodriguez Bicknell**, Soulful Books is a publishing home for purpose-driven writers who are ready to bring their message to life with clarity, confidence, and authenticity.

From manuscript readiness through design, formatting, distribution setup, and launch support, we guide you through each step of the publishing process—so your book is produced professionally, aligned with your vision, and ready to reach the readers it's meant for. Writing with us is more than creating a book—it's a meaningful milestone that turns your story into a lasting legacy.

Your story matters. Let's bring it to life and create a lasting legacy.

Learn more at SandraRodriguezBicknell.com

AFFIRMATIONS

Self-Confidence Affirmation

I know that I have the ability to achieve the object of my definite purpose in life, therefore, I demand of myself persistent, continuous action towards its achievement. I realize the dominating thoughts of my mind will eventually reproduce themselves into outward, physical action, gradually transforming themselves into physical reality. I know that any desire I persistently hold in my mind will eventually seek expression through some practical means of obtaining the object back of it. As such, I have formulated a clear picture in my mind's eye of what I wish to achieve and I will never stop working until I have developed sufficient self confidence for its attainment. I fully realize that no wealth or position can long endure unless built upon truth and justice, so I will engage in no transaction that will not benefit all whom it affects. I will commit this affirmation to memory and repeat it along with full faith that it will gradually influence my thoughts and actions, thereby becoming a self confident and successful person.

Success Affirmation

I now let go of worn out conditions and worn out things. divine order is established in my mind, body and affairs. behold. I make all things new. My seeming impossible good now comes to pass the unexpected now happens. Endless good now comes to me in endless ways. I am harmonious, poised & magnetic. I now draw to myself my own. My power is God's power and is irresistible. Divine order is now established in my mind, body and affairs. I see clearly and act quickly, and my greatest expectations come to pass in a miraculous way. The tide of destiny has turned and everything comes my way. I banish the past and now live in the wonderful now, where happy surprises come to me. each day. I have a magical work in a magical way, I give magical service for magical pay. the genius within me is now released. I now fulfill my destiny. I make friends with hindrances, and every obstacle becomes a stepping stone. Everything in the universe, visible and invisible is working to bring me my own. I give thanks that the walls of Jericho fall down and all lack, limitation and failure are wiped out of my consciousness.

I am now on the Royal Road of success. Happiness and abundance, all traffic goes my way. There are no obstacles in divine mind therefore there is nothing to obstruct my good. All obstacles now vanish from my pathway. Doors fly open, gates are lifted and I enter the kingdom of fulfillment under grace. Rhythm, harmony and balance are now established in my mind, body and affairs. Men's will is powerless to interfere with God's will. God's will is now done in my mind, body and affairs. God's plan for me is permanent and cannot be budged. I am true to my heavenly vision. The divine plan of my life now takes shape in definite, concrete experiences leading to my heart's desire. I now draw from the universal substance with irresistible power and determination, that which is mine by divine right. I do not resist my current situation. I put it in the hands of infinite love and wisdom. Let the divine idea now come to pass. My good now flows to me in a steady, unbroken, ever increasing stream of success, happiness and abundance. I am as necessary to God as he is to me for I am the channel to bring his plans to pass. I do not limit God by seeing limitations in myself. With God and myself, all things are possible. Every man is a golden link in the chain of my good. God cannot fail So I cannot fail. The Warrior Within me has already won. Thy kingdom Come in me, Thy will be done in me, and my affairs.

Prosperity Affirmation

I now release the gold mine within me. I am linked with an endless golden stream of prosperity which comes to me under grace in perfect ways. My God is a God of plenty, and I now receive all that I desire or require and more. All that is mine by divine right is now released and reaches me in great avalanches of abundance under grace and miraculous ways, my supply is endless, inexhaustible and immediate and comes to me under grace in perfect ways. I give thanks that the millions which are mine by divine right now pour in and pile up under grace and perfect ways. Unexpected doors fly open. Unexpected channels are free and endless avalanches of abundance are poured out upon me under grace and perfect ways. I spend money under direct inspiration, wisely and fearlessly, knowing my supply is endless and immediate. I am fearless in letting money go out knowing God is my immediate and endless supply.

I am one with the infinite riches of my subconscious mind. It is my right to be rich, happy, and successful. Money flows to me freely, copiously and endlessly and I give thanks. I am forever conscious of my true worth. I give my talent freely and I am wonderfully blessed financially. It is wonderful!

Well Being Affirmation

My nerves are in perfect order all over my body. They obey my will and I have a great nerve force. I am breathing deeply and quietly, and the air goes into every cell of my lungs, which are in perfect condition. My blood is purified and made clean. My heart is beating strongly and steadily, and my circulation is perfect, even to the extremities. My stomach and bowels perform their work perfectly. My food is digested and assimilated, and my body rebuilt and nourished. My liver, kidneys and bladder each perform their several functions without pain or strain. I am perfectly well. My body is resting, my mind is quiet and my soul is at peace. I have no anxiety about financial or other matters. God who is within me, is also in all things I want, impelling them towards me. all that I want is already given to me. I have no anxiety about my health, for I am perfectly well. I have no worry or fear whatever. I rise above all temptations to moral evil. I cast out all greed, selfishness and narrow personal ambition. I do not hold envy, malice or enmity towards any living soul. I will follow no course of action which is not in accord with my highest ideals. I am right and I will do right.

Divine Order Affirmation

Divine order takes charge of my life today and every day. All things work for good for me today. This is a new and wonderful day for me. There will never be another day like this one. I am divinely guided all day long and whatever I do will prosper. Divine love surrounds me, unfolds me and enwraps me and I go forth in peace. Whenever my attention wonders away from that which is good and constructive, I will immediately bring it back to the contemplation of that which is lovely and of good rapport. I am a spiritual and mental magnet, attracting to myself all things which bless and prosper me. I am going to be a great success in all of my undertakings today. I am definitely going to be happy all day long.

Acceptance Affirmation

All is right with the world. It is perfect and advancing to completion. I will contemplate the facts of social, political and industrial life only from this high viewpoint. Behold, it is all very good. I will see all human beings, all my acquaintances, friends, neighbors and the members of my own household, in the same way. They are all good. Nothing is wrong with the universe. Nothing can be wrong but my own personal attitude, and henceforth I keep that right my whole trust is in God. I will obey my soul and be true to that within me that is highest. I will search within for the pure idea of right in all things, and when I find it, I will express it in my outward life. I will abandon everything I have outgrown for the best I can think. I will have the highest thoughts concerning all my relationships and my manner and action shall express these thoughts.